CAE Result

Workbook Resource Pack with key

Kathy Gude
Lynda Edwards

OXFORD
UNIVERSITY PRESS

OXFORD
UNIVERSITY PRESS

Great Clarendon Street, Oxford OX2 6DP

Oxford University Press is a department of the University of Oxford.
It furthers the University's objective of excellence in research, scholarship,
and education by publishing worldwide in

Oxford New York

Auckland Cape Town Dar es Salaam Hong Kong Karachi
Kuala Lumpur Madrid Melbourne Mexico City Nairobi
New Delhi Shanghai Taipei Toronto

With offices in

Argentina Austria Brazil Chile Czech Republic France Greece
Guatemala Hungary Italy Japan Poland Portugal Singapore
South Korea Switzerland Thailand Turkey Ukraine Vietnam

OXFORD and OXFORD ENGLISH are registered trade marks of
Oxford University Press in the UK and in certain other countries

ACKNOWLEDGEMENTS

The authors and publishers would like to thank Tom Bradbury, Petrina Cliff,
and the advanced students of EF International Language School, London.

*The authors and publisher are grateful to those who have given permission to reproduce
the following extracts and adaptations of copyright material*: p4–5 abridged extract
from 'Better and Better' by Caroline Righton from *The Guardian* 23 April 2005
© 2005 by Caroline Righton. p8 abridged extract from 'What are friends
for?' by Jenni Russell from *The Guardian G2* 24 January 2005 © Guardian
Newspapers Limited 2005. p10–11 abridged extract from 'Sled Time Story'
by Jenny Diski from *The Observer* 30 January 2005. Reproduced by kind
permission of AP Watt Ltd on behalf of Jenny Diski. p16 abridged extract
from 'Now NASA looks to change Earth into a garden of Earthly delights'
by Robin McKie from *The Observer* 28 March 2004 © Guardian Newspapers
Limited 2004. p17 Extract from *Consider Phlebas* by Iain M. Banks 1987,
reproduced by kind permission of Little Brown Books Group. p21 abridged
extract from 'The Power of Darkness' by Hugh Wilson from *The Guardian* 15
March 2005 © Guardian Newspapers Limited 2005. p24–25 abridged extract
from 'Take The Plunge' by Dottie Monaghan from *Woman and Home* magazine
© Woman and Home/IPC & Syndication. p28 abridged extract from 'The
Animal Olympics' from *The Daily Express* 11 July 2005 © Express Newspapers
2005. p29 abridged extract from 'Among The Giants' by Sebastião Salgado
from *The Guardian* 7 May 2005. Reproduced by kind permission of the author.
p31 abridged extract from 'Human Body Has No Limits, Says Texas A & M
Professor' from the website www.tamu.edu. Reproduced by kind permission
of the author. p34 abridged extract from 'Out to Lunch' by Bibi Van der Zee
from *The Guardian G2* 24 January 2005 © Guardian Newspapers Limited 2005.
p36–37 abridged extract from 'I need a heroine' by Tanya Gold from *The
Guardian* 1 July 2005 © Guardian Newspapers Limited 2005. p41 'Brilliant
Idea: mirror lights up village' by John Follain, *The Sunday Times*, Wednesday
12th November 2006. Reproduced by kind permission of NI Syndication. p44
abridged extract from 'Is This The Death Of The Big Easy?' by Peter Sheridan
from *The Daily Express* 3 September 2005 © Express Newspapers 2005. p45
'The Relic of Mary Rose'. Permission was granted by Genesis Publications
Ltd. p50–51 abridged extract from 'We're funny in the brain' by Jerome Burn
from *The Times* 30 October 2004 © The Times 2004. p56–57 abridged extract
from 'Families and other criminals' by Suzanne Yager from *The Telegraph*
April 2005 © Daily Telegraph 2005. p60 abridged extract from 'Tough Love'
by Rebecca Smithers from *The Guardian* 21 June 2005 © Guardian Newspapers
Limited 2005. p64–65 abridged extract from 'The Tiger's Teeth' by Jonathan
Watts from *The Guardian* 25 May 2005 © Guardian Newspapers Limited
2005. p70 abridged extract from 'The biggest flatpack table and chair ever'
by Dan Carrier from *Camden New Journal* 16 June 2005. Reproduced by kind
permission of the author. p71 Jacket blurb from *The Dark Tower V11: The
Dark Tower* by Stephen King © 2004. Reproduced by permission of Hodder
& Stoughton Limited. p77 abridged extract from 'Feel-good factor but will
it save the planet?' by John Vidal and Paul Brown from *The Guardian* 20 May
2005 © Guardian Newspapers Limited 2005.

Sources: p40 www.bodyoptimise.com; p69 'Free Enterprise' by Donnie
Walker from www.bbc.co.uk; p74 'Learn about modern art periods' from
www.soyouwanna.com; p81 'Battle of the bag' by Caroline Williams from
The New Scientist 11 September 2004.

*The publishers would like to thank the following for their kind permission to reproduce
photographs*: Alamy pp10/11 (Bryan and Cherry Alexander Photography), 15
(Andrew Morse), 16b (The Print Collector), 20b (Brian and Cherry Alexander
Photography), 28bc (blinkwinkel), 28bl (Walt Stearns/Stephen Frink
Collection), 48 (Lebrecht Music and Arts Photo Library), 60c (Martin Hunter),
70 (Shangara Singh), 76bl (David Gordon), 80 (Pictor International/Image
State), 93tl (Ian Miles-Flashpoint Pictures), 94cl (John Powell Photographer),
96br (Popperfoto), 96tr (Henry Westheim); Corbis UK Ltd pp11 (Setboun),
14c (Jose Luis Pelaez Inc), 14b (Otto Rogge) 16t, (NASA), 21 (Images.com),
24/25 (Mark M.Lawrence), 25 (Stephen Frink), 26l (Bill Ross), 28tc (Abbie
Enock/Travel Ink), 28tl (Kevin Schafer), 28tr (Tom Brakefield), 29 (Tim
Graham/Sygma), 35l (Helen King), 34t (Comstock Select), 34b (David Ashley)
36b (Sunset Boulevard), 41 (Ray Juno), 44 (Bettmann), 45r (Mimmo Jodice),
47 (Ludovic Maisant), 49 (Keren Su), 50 (© LWA-Stephen Welstead), 51
(Simon Marcus), 60t, 60b (Image 100), 72 (Tom & Dee Ann McCarthy), 74r
(Burstein Collection), 75 (Lucy Nicholson/Reuters), 76t (Gideon Mendel),
92r (China Photo/Reuters), 92cl, 92l (Jim Bourg/Reuters), 93br (Roger De
La Harpe/Gallo Images), 93tr (Michael Freeman), 94bl (Tom Stewart), 94br
(david Pollack), 94cr (Eric K.K. Yu), 94tl (Toma stewart), 94tr (James Leynse),
96bl (K.M.Westermann), 96tr (Frank Trapper); Getty Images pp5 (Karen
Moskowitz/The Image Bank), 9 (West Rock/Taxi), 17r (Jack Ambrose/Stone),
17l (John Lamb/Stone) 20t, 33 (Philip and Karen Smith/Stone) 46, 58 (question
mark/David Dacosta/Stock Illustration Source); Genesis Publications p45l;
Guardian Newspapers p8l & r (Linda Nylind 2005); Hodder and Stoughton
71r; iStockphoto pp64l (Daniel Brunner), 64/65t (Stefan Klein), 74l (Dave
White); Linographic pp64/65b, 69 (all); NASA p16l (Pat Rawlings); Orion
Publishing Group p57; Oxford University Press pp27, 40t; Photolibrary
pp28br (Mary Plage), 76/77 (Peter J.Robinson); Punchstock pp14t (Blend
Images), 52 (Debra Spina Dixon/Photodisc), 71l (Digital Vision); Rex Features
p54 (David James); Ronald Grant Archive pp36c (Warner Bros), 37, 40b; Still
Pictures p81 (Emmanuel Vialet); Superstock p34c; Transworld Publishers Ltd
p56; Universal Studios p61.

Illustrations by: Gill Button pp13, 53; Melvyn Evans pp19, 59, 73, 79

Pages 97–101 reproduced with the kind permission of Cambridge ESOL.

What are you like?

Reading Part 3 Multiple choice

1 Read the article quickly and decide which sentence (a, b or c) is the best summary.

   a Dealing with problems in your life.
   b Finding out how to take things easy.
   c Learning to be more positive.

2 Read the text again and for questions 1–5, choose the answer (A, B, C or D) which you think fits best.

1 What does the writer advise people to do before getting up in the morning?

   A Calmly contemplate their day ahead.
   B Organise their routine to maximise their time.
   C Decide which undesirable activity they could dispense with.
   D Reject the idea of having to fulfil their obligations successfully.

Better and **better**

TAKE A COUPLE OF MINUTES to lie still in bed and reflect on the day ahead. Do you feel cheerful or fed up, excited or bored? Or do you, perhaps, feel nothing? Go on, prod your subconscious to consider your
5 situation. Unless you get pleasure from living a passive and non-eventful life, having a non-committal attitude can actually be as bad as being pessimistic. So if, as you walk yourself through the events of the day ahead, you feel pretty average about things, then try and aim
10 higher. It will mean that you get much more out of life. So there you are, lying in bed. Picture yourself showering, making breakfast, catching the bus, attending meetings, shopping, cooking supper, watching TV and finally getting into bed. Did your spirits sink at the thought of any of it?
15 If so, pluck what it was out of the timetable and examine it more closely. Is it a must-do, non-negotiable event? For instance, you may not mind the idea of going to work but hate your job or the daily commute. Find out what options you have to make changes or find alternatives.
20 In the meantime, come up with a strong and confident affirming statement about the person you wish to be and the way you wish to tackle these life challenges.

Once you have a clear picture of the things in your life that make you feel low, either eliminate, minimise or
25 improve them and the way you manage them. If getting everyone organised in the morning is a nightmare, you need to apply some lateral thought to the process. Encourage everybody to help with the morning routine. Make everyone responsible for some parts of their own
30 organisation. If everyone is leading busy lives in the household, it makes no sense for one person to be a martyr. Be realistic about your own stamina and stress limits and appreciate the importance of keeping yourself fit and happy. Agree new regimes with family members
35 or housemates as a sensible training exercise, and stick with it until everyone takes their equal share. Instead of feeling miserable about your chores and responsibilities, adopt a positive approach and acknowledge that they are an essential component of life.

2 The writer suggests dealing with difficult aspects of our home lives by

 A freeing up more time to handle them more effectively.
 B delegating some responsibilities to others.
 C learning to control stress by taking more exercise.
 D asking for outside help to relieve pressures.

3 The writer initially implies that adopting a realistic attitude towards life can

 A have a counterproductive effect on our lives.
 B encourage us to look on the bright side of life.
 C enable us to find solutions to our problems.
 D help us be more analytical in our approach to life.

4 The writer justifies having a positive outlook on the day by saying it will

 A make the outcome of our day more predictable.
 B help us blank out the less desirable events in our lives.
 C give us renewed energy to face up to problems in life.
 D reinforce our appreciation of what makes life worthwhile.

5 According to the writer, how should we react to having had a bad day?

 A Focus on the one positive thing that happened, however insignificant.
 B Try to communicate our feelings about it to another person in a positive way.
 C Tell ourselves it is perfectly acceptable to feel down after a day like that.
 D Stay positive and believe that tomorrow will be a better day.

40 Pessimism, doubt and negativity can often disguise themselves as realism. Facing up to the facts can sometimes be healthy but it's essential not to poison hope and optimism with negative thoughts. Observing how you think is vital. You really need to tune into
45 hearing those negative waves as soon as they start and see a more positive alternative view. To find this perspective, you may need to examine closely the experience or subject of your attention. Be curious and interested in life, the things and the people that make
50 up your day. Be resolute that you will find a positive in everything and everyone.

The logical rationale for having a positive attitude is compelling. Nobody knows for sure what each day will bring and whether its end will mark a personal triumph
55 or disaster. Make yourself work out what good things will happen. Today could be the day you meet your soul mate, or when you are praised or promoted. Carry a list and photographs of things in your life that are rewarding or make you feel happy. This can include
60 loved ones, favourite flowers, song tracks, a cutting from a newspaper that made you laugh, or a theatre ticket that reminds you of a wonderful occasion. If you need reminding that good things do happen, take this collection out and relive fond memories and thoughts.

65 Even if today has been a bad day, you needn't go to bed depressed because your optimism didn't pay off. Why? Well, because tomorrow is another day. In the same way that a single look or a sour comment can instantly kill a feeling, so a bubble of optimism arising from even the
70 most minor triumph will eventually get bigger if you refuse to let yourself look on the dark side. That is the great thing about life.

Vocabulary

Feelings

1 Put these words into a suitable category below. Check your answers in your dictionary. Then use them to complete sentences a–g.

depressed	confident	cheerful	fed up
curious	pessimistic	resolute	optimistic
moody	realistic		

Positive: ....

....

Negative: ....

....

Neutral: ....

....

a I'm .... with everyone asking me to do things for them all the time. Nobody ever says thank you or helps me.

b Bob has a rather .... attitude towards the future of our planet. He's convinced global warming will destroy the planet very soon.

c We must be .... and do everything possible to improve the transport facilities in the town.

d Zeb seems very .... He wasn't nervous about making that speech to the whole college.

e You're not being very .... about our plans for the summer. We just couldn't afford to go on holiday to a place like that.

f You never know how Ann will feel – happy, sad – she can be very ....

g I'm .... to know how many students passed the exam, aren't you?

Meanings of *get*

2 Match the expressions in italics in a–h with one of the meanings in brackets.

a If you want to *get more out of* life, try to be more organised. (create or invent more from/extract or obtain more from)

b I'd like to *get out of* going to the party tonight but I don't see how I can. (avoid doing something/persuade someone not to do something)

c I'm really struggling with this grammar. I just don't *get* it. (understand/like)

d We ought to be going home. It's *getting on for* midnight. (past/nearly)

e It's no good *getting* upset about what happened. There's nothing you can do about it now. (making/becoming)

f The students *get on with* each other very well. (make progress/have a good relationship)

g I think it's time we *got down* to doing our homework. (finished/began)

h This argument is *getting us nowhere*. Let's just agree to disagree. (achieving nothing/leading us in the wrong direction)

3 Complete sentences a–g using a suitable expression with *get* in the correct form. Then use your dictionary to find two more expressions with *get* and note their meaning.

a Do you .... Kate? I really don't know her.

b We need to .... doing all the jobs in the house that we haven't done for ages.

c This consultation process is .... It's virtually impossible to please everybody.

d It's .... 6 o'clock. Great! It's nearly time to finish work and go home!

e I want to try to .... college, you know, join some clubs or learn a new language.

f Try not to .... offended by what Mary said. I'm sure she didn't really mean it.

g How can we .... visiting the Browns this weekend? I'd rather stay at home!

Grammar

Review of verb patterns

1 Complete conversations 1–6 by putting the verb in brackets in the correct form.

1 A: One of my colleagues wanted me .... (buy) a mobile phone like hers.

   B: But yours is quite new. I really object to .... (change) something for the sake of it.

2 A: We could put off .... (make) a decision about installing machinery until next year.

   B: That might mean we need to resort to .... (spend) a huge amount on maintaining the existing machinery.

3 A: Has it always been company policy to avoid .... (give) a refund on sales goods?

   B: Yes. You can issue a credit note but you must insist on .... (see) the receipt.

4 A: I don't recall .... (receive) any notification about the change in dates.

   B: I'm afraid it was a last minute amendment. I do apologise for .... (not/inform) you.

5 A: The Wrights never stop .... (boast) about their children's achievements.

   B: Perhaps you ought to .... (mention) the fact that they have already told you!

6 A: Bill can't stand .... (commute) for three hours every day.

   B: Maybe you should advise him .... (look) for a job closer to home?

2 Complete these sentences using a suitable verb below in the infinitive form with or without *to*.

▮ strike   complete   feel   provide
   solve   accept   enter

a Several residents heard someone .... the building in the early hours of the morning.

b The management refuse .... responsibility for any damage to property on the premises.

c Under the terms of the contract, we agree .... the work in a period of three weeks.

d The letter was written in such an aggressive tone that it made me .... angry.

e Sam's tutor offered .... him with some extra help with his thesis.

f Can anyone help .... this confusion about transportation costs?

g The baggage handlers at the airport threatened .... if their demands were not met.

3 Match the sentence halves using the prepositions below and the correct form of the verb in brackets. Three of the prepositions are <u>not</u> needed.

▮ at   for   on   of   from   by

a Please don't blame me …

b I can't believe Anne's supervisor actually accused her …

c The police praised everyone …

d Most hotels try to discourage guests …

e Voters will never forgive the government …

f Officials tried to prevent the spectators …

g That scruffy old rucksack reminds me …

1 (smoke) in their bedrooms.

2 (forget) what you should have remembered yourself.

3 (not/live) up to their election promises.

4 (steal) her own office stationery.

5 (rush) onto the pitch at the end of the game.

6 (travel) across Europe when I was a student.

7 (not/panic) during the bomb scare.

Listening Part 4 Multiple matching

1 Read the instructions and questions for 2, which are about people discussing friendship. Which statements reflect your own opinions or experiences?

2 🎧 Listen to five short extracts and complete the exam task.

For 1–5, choose from A–H the people's attitudes towards friendships.

A The only people I feel I can make demands on are my friends.
B I think I can honestly say that I have never really had a best friend.
C I expect my friends to place our friendship above everything.
D We often give friends a one-sided impression of our true selves.
E Friends are people you can invite to a dinner party at the last minute.
F I always take advantage of opportunities to meet people.
G My friendships mean far more to me than even my job.
H I socialise with people of a similar background to myself.

Speaker 1 [ ] [1]

Speaker 2 [ ] [2]

Speaker 3 [ ] [3]

Speaker 4 [ ] [4]

Speaker 5 [ ] [5]

For 6–10, choose from A–H what upsets the people about friendships.

A not being able to rely on friends in times of trouble
B being bothered by someone who won't accept the friendship is over
C constantly being forced to make new friends
D realising that your friendship is no longer of any value
E dealing with friends' emotional problems
F losing touch with people who have been your friends since childhood
G being let down by friends at work
H knowing their position in the group is what matters to your friends

Speaker 1 [ ] [6]

Speaker 2 [ ] [7]

Speaker 3 [ ] [8]

Speaker 4 [ ] [9]

Speaker 5 [ ] [10]

Use of English   Part 3 Word formation

1 Read the article below about interviews. How does the author advise people to perfect their interview technique?

   a in front of a mirror
   b with someone they know well
   c with an expert in the field

2 Read the text again and complete gaps 1–10 with words formed from those in capitals below.

Preparing for your first interview

Before going to an interview, it is (0) ....**advisable**.... to go through a mock interview. This will give you the opportunity to try out your technique and answers live. It is also a chance to receive feedback that is (1) .... in guiding you towards improving your interview style and general (2) .... Just one mock interview will result in a (3) .... improvement in your interview skills. Why? For the same reason that a (4) .... doesn't exist while it is still on paper or floating in your head. It only exists when you give it (5) .... The first time you give it in front of an audience, it will come out nothing like the one you prepared.

It is the same with being interviewed. It is not enough to look at a question and say, 'Yeah, I know the answer to that one'. You need to practise your answer live; this is not the time to talk to yourself in front of a mirror. Seek out a (6) .... and have the session videotaped. Then you will have two opinions – the interviewer's and your own. You will find you get a completely different (7) .... when listening to yourself than when you are watching yourself saying something. Just as your voice always sounds different on tape, so do your (8) .... You will be glad the image is captured on tape and not in a potential employer's mind. For maximum effect, you should (9) .... your answers and go through a second mock interview. This should help with any (10) .... and give you more confidence for the real interview.

0	ADVISE	4	SPEAK	8	RESPOND
1	BENEFIT	5	ORAL	9	VISIT
2	PRESENT	6	PROFESSION	10	EASE
3	NOTICE	7	IMPRESS		

Part 4 Gapped sentences

3 Think of one word only which can be used appropriately in all three sentences. The word is an answer from the text above.

The bride's brother gave an excellent .... at the wedding reception.
We use idioms much more often in .... than in writing.
She had a really high temperature and her .... was unclear.

4 Write the three different definitions for the answer in 3. Check the accuracy of your definitions in your dictionary. Then write another example sentence for each definition.

Customs and traditions

Reading Part 2 Gapped text

1 Read the text and paragraphs A–G quickly and find out:
a who the Sami are.
b what annual custom the writer takes part in.
c if the writer enjoyed the experience.

2 Read the whole text again and choose from the paragraphs A–G the one which fits each gap (1–6). There is one extra paragraph which you do not need to use.

ARCTIC ADVENTURES

I wanted to spend a few days brooding under the midday moon. A heated log cabin and maybe a sauna, in Sweden's far north, above the Arctic circle. And I would meditate on the loss of light and the
5 loneliness, in a drawn-out, snowy, winter world where the sun never shines. And that's what I said when the editor asked what I'd like to write about and I was quickly packed off to Övre Soppero with photographer Mark. 'Oh, it's never dark up here,'
10 our host Per-Nils Päiviö insisted when we met him and his wife, Britt-Marie, who was preparing a reindeer stew with lingonberry sauce.

The next two days and nights in the warmth of the cabin and the traditional circular hut covered in
15 turf, with wood-burning stoves – and yes, a sauna – were cosy enough. Informative, too, as – along with a breakfast of pancakes – I was given a thorough education in the ancient and barely altered life of the reindeer-herding Sami people of northern
20 Sweden. Just as I was beginning to relax, I found myself being introduced to 'my' reindeer. I was handed the reins along with some sparse instructions: pull left for faster, right for stop.

Tonight Per-Nils was taking us by snowmobile to
25 the huts by the network of corrals where the families lived over the three-day round-up. But he, Mark and I were spending the night in a lavvu, guarding the reindeer. Back home I had discovered that 'lavvu', which had appeared on
30 my itinerary, meant a tent. I imagined a nice, warm tourist tent. Now, 'spending the night' began to ring alarm bells.

Somehow, I survived, stiff and a little mad with lack of sleep. Then the round-up began. All the families revved up their snowmobiles and spread
35 out in a mysterious pattern, surrounding the reindeer. Dogs barked, people shouted to each other in the grey light, and 7,000 reindeer ran in the desired direction: into a large corral. They were herded by a long line of people on foot
40 towards the narrow passage; then 70 or so animals were funnelled into the small circular rodeo space which had gates to 'family' paddocks radiating off it.

A
But for me, the best thing was that it had the Hotel
Ralleran, an old, wooden building devotedly restored,
75 and a shrine to simplicity and comfort. It had
beautiful, pale-timbered walls, wooden floors, light,
space and the most comfortable bed I have ever
slept in and at last a jacuzzi.

B
I sat in the family paddock by a fire of seven-foot logs
80 and choked on woodsmoke. 'Ah', a fur-encased elderly
lady laughed. 'The smoke follows you. It means that
you will be rich.' Or so her daughter translated. What
she was probably saying was: 'Who is this stranger?'

C
Dinner was delicious and warming, and marked our
85 introduction to Swedish Lapland as guests of the
Sami, the indigenous people who were here long
before the Swedes, Norwegians, Finns and Russians
arrived. 'Snow. Northern lights. The moon for two
weeks every month. You can go out in the forest in
90 the middle of December and you hardly need a torch',
he commented. Despite my initial reservation, I was
becoming intrigued by this dark world and was
actually keen to start our 'adventure'.

D
Yet they showed a demonstrable desire to keep their
95 Sami heritage, not as a museum exhibit but an actual
existence. It's one reason why the Sami are inviting
small groups of visitors to share something of their
traditions and so they can try to sustain their
reindeer-herding way of life.

E
100 My fears turned out to be justified. The Sami version
of a tepee had a layer of reindeer skins over the bare,
snow-covered, and where I was sleeping, lumpy earth.
The fifteen-centimetre gap around the bottom was
apparently to let the fresh air in. I spent most of the
105 time perched on my elbows, staring at the embers of
the fire in the centre.

F
The reindeer took over immediately, either sauntering
along or racing his best mate. My performance did
lose the respect of the other guides, but thankfully
110 they were kind about it and excitely started talking
about tomorrow's agenda. They had brought together
the 7,000 reindeer of the whole district, and
tomorrow we would be able to participate in the
great annual separation of the herds into family
115 groups. This is done according to the signs on the ears
of each yearling calf and to allocate the winter
grazing. Spending a day with 7,000 reindeer –
naturally, I was thrilled!

G
My job was to stand to one side and head off the
120 stragglers and escapees. This is done by flapping the
arms up and down (a good way of keeping warm) and
hooting. Even the most desultory of flaps will
persuade a wayward reindeer – as I discovered to my
relief – to get back into the crowd.

45 I declined to wrestle with a reindeer, but Mark
put down his camera and became a veritable
Sami by grabbing it and shouting, 'It's one of
ours', as he was dragged across the corral floor.
Having no interest in honour, I begged for a bed
50 with walls around it that night, and maybe even
with a jacuzzi.

We had another magical, frozen ride back on the
snowmobile and then a car to Kiruna, the town
that contains the Sami parliament and is home
55 to the Swedish iron ore mine. The mine has
contracted and has utterly changed the
traditional herding land, and is part of what
threatens the Sami way of life.

5 ☐

After a day off, I visited some Sami pupils at a
60 local school. They take some of their lessons in
their own language and learn about skills and
traditions that are rapidly being forgotten. All the
youngsters were looking to the future and making
plans for their lives beyond reindeer herding.

6 ☐

65 Even the likes of me can recognise how
privileged I was to participate in that. And we
were told that the extra hands can even be
useful: Mark apparently was an asset, not just a
gawking outsider. Me? Well, now I've warmed up
70 a bit, I am very grateful to have had such an
extraordinary experience. All I can hope is that I
didn't make life too difficult for my patient hosts.

Vocabulary

Words with similar meanings (1)

1 Match one word from each pair in a–e with the definition provided and then write a definition for the other word. Use your dictionary to help you.

   a imaginary/imaginative
   having or showing new and exciting ideas

   ....

   b exhausting/exhaustive
   making you feel very tired

   ....

   c conscience/conscientious
   part of your mind that tells you whether your actions are right or wrong

   ....

   d satisfying/satisfactory
   good enough for a particular purpose

   ....

   e sensible/sensitive
   aware of and able to understand other people and their feelings

   ....

2 Use words from 1 to complete these sentences.

   a Fortunately, your performance was .... and you passed the exam.
   b Samson is a very .... writer and always constructs an intricate and fascinating plot.
   c The government's survey into unemployment is the most .... document of its kind.
   d I can't believe Chris cheated in the exam! Doesn't he have a .... ?
   e Our school is .... to problems facing new students and we aim to support them fully.

Compound nouns

3 Circle the one word on the right which <u>cannot</u> be combined with a–e to form a compound noun. Then scan through the entries for a–e in your dictionary to find more compound nouns.

   a hand   book/shake/bar/basin
   b film   crew/goer/picture/script
   c news   agent/flash/data/reader
   d side   effect/mark/track/street
   e work   hour/shop/place/out

4 Make compound nouns by matching a–e with 1–5. There may be more than one answer. Check your ideas in a dictionary.

   a take   1 through
   b turn   2 over
   c set   3 out
   d hand   4 back
   e break   5 down

5 Use the compound nouns you formed in 4 to complete these sentences. Then say what each compound noun means in the context of a–h.

   a The surprisingly low .... at the tennis tournament was due to torrential rain.
   b An unsuccessful .... bid was made by an unknown investor last year.
   c Research into hereditary illness has resulted in a welcome .... for scientists.
   d A .... will be distributed to all students at the end of the lecture.
   e Unfortunately, there has been a temporary .... in the peace negotiations.
   f It is reputed that the oil company has an annual .... of forty million dollars.
   g The .... of power to the newly elected government took place yesterday.
   h There has been a .... at the prison – three inmates are thought to have escaped.

Grammar

Gerunds and infinitives

1 Complete gaps 1–8 with the correct form of the verbs below. You may need to add a preposition.

> ■ be   waste   establish   cope   send
>   travel   go   expand

Tim wasn't looking forward 1 .... on his first business trip to Latvia in the middle of winter. He wasn't very keen 2 .... in icy conditions and he'd never been very good at 3 .... with cold temperatures. In any case, he didn't believe 4 .... time making personal visits when a phone call or email would do just as well. He objected 5 .... told what to do, but his boss had insisted 6 .... him there for a brief meeting. The company had been thinking 7 .... into that part of the world for some time and had already succeeded 8 .... contacts in Central and Eastern Europe.

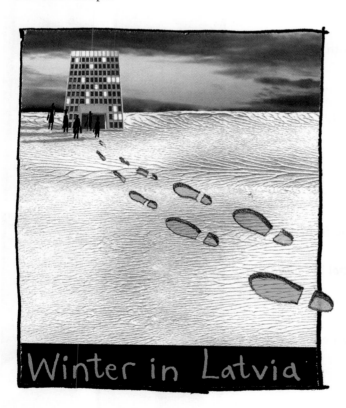

Winter in Latvia

2 Match sentence halves a–f with 1–6 and put the verbs in brackets in the correct form.

a Did Sally actually manage …
b Is it true that Sam threatened …
c What do you hope …
d I don't think we should risk …
e Would you prefer …
f The accused man denied …

1 (do) in ten years' time?
2 (convince) Andrea to watch that horror film?
3 (drive) to the airport in case there's a traffic jam.
4 (have) a vegetarian dish for your main course?
5 (resign) if he wasn't given a salary increase?
6 (steal) the money but no one believed him.

Relative clauses

3 Combine the sentences in a–g using a relative pronoun and, where necessary, a preposition.

a This is the old car. William used it to travel all over Europe.
b The new train can reach speeds of 300 km per hour. The train's design is certainly innovative.
c The Welsh mountains are very beautiful. I spent most of my childhood there.
d We met other employees. Most had been with the company for a few years.
e Winning the World Cup was one of those wonderful moments. You feel perfectly happy.
f The film star is the subject of much gossip. She will be at the premiere in New York tomorrow.
g The accident happened. We cannot explain it.

Listening

Part 1 Short extracts

1 Answer these questions which relate to the extracts in 2 below.

    a What are the most popular traditional dishes in your country?
    b Were there any particular customs from your childhood that you enjoyed?
    c Which are the most popular tourist attractions in your country?

2 🎧 Read questions 1–6 below before you listen to the three different extracts. Then listen and choose the answer (A, B or C) which fits best according to what you hear.

You hear part of an interview with a woman who is writing a series of guides about traditional food.

1 What information do the guides give?
    A introductions to the leading chefs of the area
    B the reasons why certain meals became popular
    C details of locally grown produce used in dishes

2 What is the writer's reason for writing the guides?
    A to teach a new generation of cooks
    B to develop her experience as a writer
    C to help tourists find authentic traditional food

You hear two people talking about customs from their childhood.

3 What do the speakers believe about the Tooth Fairy?
    A It can only visit when you sleep.
    B It is a purely British custom.
    C It helps a new tooth grow.

4 The woman continued the custom with her children because
    A children's teeth are important.
    B children should have beliefs like this.
    C customs shouldn't be broken.

You hear part of an interview with a tour guide from Australia.

5 The tour guide describes Ayers Rock as special because it is
    A a different colour from normal rock.
    B bigger than any other rock on earth.
    C a major visitor attraction for Australia.

6 Visitors are not allowed to climb Ayers Rock because
    A its history should be respected.
    B tours make it overcrowded.
    C there isn't a safe track.

Use of English

Part 2 Open cloze

1 Read the text below quickly, ignoring the gaps, and find out how the Japanese festival started.

2 For questions 1–15, read the text again and think of the word which best fits each gap.

STATUES OF SAPPORO

The capital of Japan's northernmost island attracts a cavalcade of visitors (0) ....**every**.... year at the beginning of February. (1) .... this being the coldest time of the year, visitors flock to the city, which transforms (2) .... into a winter dream world heaving with glittering figures and beautiful palaces. More than two million people come to marvel (3) .... the frosted statues.

The festival, which (4) .... extremely humble origins, is today a high-profile international event. It began in 1950 (5) .... a couple of young students fashioned six snow statues in Odori Park. Five years (6) .... , members of Sapporo's Defence Force sowed the seeds (7) .... the now world-famous festival by building the first statue, which was megalithic in (8) .... proportions. Snow sculpting might sound (9) .... one of those skills best suited to the school playground, but it actually takes a (10) .... of patience and artistic talent to form these snow giants. First, a wooden structure is built. Large blocks of snow (11) .... then cut from the ground. The blocks, (12) .... are hammered into place around the scaffolding, are then hosed down with water to freeze them into hard-as-rock mortar. It is only (13) .... that the painstaking job of sculpting the masterpiece begins.

The combined result of (14) .... this sculpting and carving is a crystal-like dreamscape of frosted versions of many famous buildings, (15) .... as the Statue of Liberty and the Leaning Tower of Pisa.

Part 5 Key word transformations

3 Rewrite the second sentence in a–d keeping the meaning the same. Use three to six words, including the word given.

a The majority of people like to observe customs and traditions.
FAVOUR
The majority of people ....
.... customs and traditions.

b We are not often invited to meetings at the college.
ACCUSTOMED
We are not ....
to meetings at the college.

c The results show attendance has risen dramatically during the last year.
IN
The results show a ....
.... during the last year.

d My sister finds commuting every day really annoying.
PUT
It's difficult for my sister ....
.... commuting every day.

Looking ahead

3

Reading

Part 1 Themed texts

1 Read the three extracts opposite quickly to find which ones mention the possibility of visiting

a an island.
b a space agency.
c outer space.

2 Read the extracts again and for questions 1–6, choose the answer (A, B, C or D) which you think fits best according to the text.

LIFE ON MARS?

B illions of years after the last seas and rivers dried up on Mars, scientists believe they may be able to restore the Red Planet to its former glory – by turning it into a blue world with streams, green fields and fresh breezes, and filling it with earthly creatures. Ultimately this
05 could even provide mankind's increasing numbers with a new home. This revolutionary scheme of 'terraforming' recently formed the focus of a major international debate hosted by America's space agency, NASA.

Terraforming has always been considered fiction but now, with a multi-billion-dollar Mars research programme drawn up by NASA, there is the
10 chance to discover the real possibilities of transforming Mars. There are many critics. Foremost among these is Paul Murdin of the Institute of Astronomy. He believes the idea of terraforming Mars is extreme but not ridiculous. 'The idea is actually a real one,' he says. 'And I find it incredible that mankind is mucking up this world at an amazing pace and, at the same
15 time, talking about doing the same to another planet.'

Other scientists feel likewise. Monica Grady, from the Natural History Museum, London, points out that Mars used to have an atmosphere, but it disappeared for reasons that are still unclear. If scientists restore Mars's atmosphere, she claims, it could just disappear again. Devastating things
20 would have been done to the planet for a temporary effect and that would certainly not be ethical. In addition to this there is the risk that terraforming would pose to any life forms that already exist on Mars. There are still a lot of scientists remaining to be convinced that terraforming Mars would be worth the massive expenditure involved and the ethical problems it would raise.

1 The idea of 'terraforming'
   A could become a reality at some point.
   B shows a dramatic change in thinking from NASA.
   C has not yet been discussed internationally.
   D initially appeared too dangerous.

2 Some scientists believe
   A we have insufficient understanding of the atmosphere on Mars.
   B creating the right atmosphere on Mars would be impossible.
   C moving life forms to Mars would be illegal.
   D terraforming Mars would destroy the planet.

CALLING ALL iNVENTORS!

25 **Do you think you can invent something … something for Space or on Earth? Did you know that many inventions have been created for use in Space?**

NASA has been responsible for creating many of our familiar and everyday objects. For example, the
30 smoke detectors in your home were initially invented to protect a shuttle crew from any toxic gases. And cordless power drills were originally made to carry out repairs to shuttles whilst in space. Many inventions that have helped Man travel and live in Space have been
35 adapted to make our lives here on Earth easier too.

Now we want to find some young inventors who could come up with ideas similar to those developed by the NASA programme. We are looking for practical ideas that could be used to make life easier on Earth … or
40 maybe to make life easier in Space! Not only will you and your friends need to come up with the idea, but you will have to think about developing and marketing the product. The prize is an amazing opportunity to visit NASA and their laboratories.

45 **HOW TO ENTER:**

Send your idea and contact details to the address below by 4 August.

You should state what the invention is, why people on Earth or in Space would benefit from it, how it could be
50 manufactured, and how you could market your product.

You must enter as a team of four friends and be aged 14–19 years old.

Invention Competition, PO Box 683, London.

Extract from a novel

55 Horza woke rolling around inside the shuttle. In the first few blurred seconds of his waking he thought he had already tumbled out of the rear door of the shuttle and was falling through the air; then his head cleared and he found himself lying spread-eagled on the floor of the rear
60 compartment, watching the blue sky outside tilt as the shuttle banked. The craft seemed to be travelling more slowly than he remembered. He could see nothing from the rear view out of the doors except blue sky, blue sea and a few puffy white clouds, so he
65 stuck his head round the side of the door.

The buffeting wind was warm, and over in the direction the shuttle was banking lay a small island. Horza looked at it incredulously. It was tiny, surrounded by smaller atolls and reefs showing pale green through
70 the shallow water, and it had a single small mountain sticking up from concentric circles of lush green vegetation and bright yellow sand. The shuttle dipped and levelled, straightening on its course for the island. Horza brought his head back in, resting the muscles
75 of his neck and shoulder after the exertion of holding his head out in the slipstream. The shuttle slowed yet more, dipping again. A slight juddering vibrated through the craft's frame.

3 A number of useful inventions have
  A come from competitions for scientists.
  B been inspired by inventions used in space.
  C encouraged an interest in space.
  D made a lot of money for the space industry.

4 For this competition, entrants need to
  A provide a model of their invention.
  B develop ideas without collaborating with others.
  C produce a detailed design of their invention.
  D explain how their invention would be sold.

5 When Horza initially woke up
  A he was confused as to where he was.
  B his vision was damaged.
  C he thought the shuttle was travelling too quickly.
  D he had a headache.

6 Why did he need to relax his neck muscles?
  A They had tightened through worry.
  B His neck had been hurt in the fall.
  C He had been leaning out of the shuttle.
  D He had slept in a strange position.

Vocabulary

Two-part phrasal verbs

1 Write nouns for phrasal verbs a–d and match them with meanings 1–5 below.

Example

burst out   *outburst* *3*

a cut back   ....
b fall down   ....
c bring up   ....
d put in   ....

1 failure of something or someone
2 raising a child
3 ~~a passing moment of anger~~
4 reduction in the amount of something
5 effort given to a project, etc.

2 Look up each of the verbs in bold (in a–f) below to find the correct particle to complete the sentences. Then match them with meanings 1–6.

a The armed robber told the cashier to **hand** *in/ on/over* the money in the till.
b What do you **make** *of/up/to* this letter from my ex-boyfriend? I'm not sure how to interpret it.
c Our elderly neighbour **passed** *off/away/up* last week so the family are selling his house.
d The manager is unable to speak at the conference tomorrow so I'm going to **stand** *in/ up/to* for him and talk to the delegates.
e I was prepared to lend my brother some money but he **turned** *back/over/down* my offer.
f Two people were **knocked** *away/off/down* by a car on a pedestrian crossing this morning.

1 take someone's place
2 give (not voluntarily)
3 hit and cause to fall
4 die
5 reject
6 understand by

3 Match the two-part phrasal verbs a–f with meanings 1–6.

a hand out   1 understand
b make out   2 distribute
c knock out   3 lose consciousness
d stand out   4 produce or make
e turn out   5 be noticeable
f pass out   6 eliminate in a competition

4 Use the correct form of the phrasal verbs from 3 to complete these sentences.

a .... leaflets in the High Street has to be one of the most boring jobs!
b There's no doubt that wearing designer clothes makes you .... in a crowd.
c How can Tim be a medical student when he .... as soon as he sees blood?
d Nobody can .... what her motives were in telling so many lies.
e Unfortunately the basketball team got .... in the first round of the tournament.
f This factory is our most productive – it .... an amazing 1,000 cars a week.

Grammar Future forms

1 Read the text about an unusual play and use the correct future form of the verbs below to complete gaps 1–8.

> sell out   know   find out   talk   meet
> perform   not effect   give

Mike Leigh is a playwright who works without a script, so the actors have to improvise. For this reason, his new play does not even have a title. But by next Friday morning, Leigh 1 .... whether his new play 2 .... with the approval of the critics or not. On Thursday evening, the cast 3 .... 'A New Play by Mike Leigh' for the first time and before an audience who 4 .... virtually nothing about it.

The fact that this is his first play for 12 years is unlikely to be a problem and 5 .... its performance at the box office. Theatregoers expect that tickets for the play's first run of performances 6 .... long before the first night, when it is hoped the play 7 .... a title. One thing, however, is certain – whatever the play is about, Leigh fans 8 .... about it for many weeks to come.

2 Which of the expressions in a–f is followed by
1   the infinitive with *to*
2   *of + ing*

a   just about
b   bound
c   on the point
d   certain
e   no possibility whatsoever
f   no chance

3 Use some of the expressions in 2 to describe your plans for the year ahead – starting from now!

Grammar Extra

Adjective and adverb order

4 The categories below show adjective order before a noun. Put the adjectives into the correct place.

> china   orange   Russian   young   rectangular
> ancient   oval   purple   Chinese   silk
> fascinating   tiny   disgusting   heavy

your opinion	....
size/weight	....
age	....
shape	....
colour	....
country of origin	....
material	....

5 Answer questions a–d about adverbs.

a   What is the correct order for the adverbial phrases of place and manner in this sentence?
The Prime Minister spoke.
(at the conference/very well)
Where could you add *on Saturday*?

b   Where would you normally put the adverb *probably* in these sentences?
Christopher knows the way to our house.
Jill doesn't know the way.

c   Which emphasising adverb would you use in these sentences?
I quite/just agree with you.
I quite/just love your new flat.

d   Where would you put the adverbs *very* or *pretty* in this sentence?
I can see the ship clearly on the horizon now.

Listening Part 3 Multiple choice

1 Look at the photos of Sally and Pete Fletcher planning a trip across Siberia on motorbikes. What difficulties do you think they may face?

2 🎧 Listen to an interview with the couple, and for questions 1–6, choose the answer (A, B, C or D) which fits best.

1 Pete says their forthcoming trip will challenge them because of the
  A kind of terrain they are crossing.
  B enormous distances they are covering.
  C means of transport they are using.
  D length of time they are taking.

2 Sally says she and Pete were motivated to go on the trip because of a
  A need for excitement.
  B lifelong ambition.
  C desire to earn money.
  D plan to write a book.

3 How does Pete feel about tackling the journey?
  A He thinks that their chances of succeeding are above average.
  B He would prefer not to talk about what might happen.
  C He's excited about the dangers they're about to experience.
  D He suspects they're about to face their toughest challenge yet.

4 According to Sally, how have friends and family reacted to their journey?
  A They have offered them their help if it should be needed.
  B They have expressed their doubts about the success of the venture.
  C They have advised them which route to take across Siberia.
  D They have encouraged them to carry on and not be dispirited.

5 They are going to ensure their safety and well-being during the journey by
  A carrying enough supplies for the whole trip.
  B avoiding routes which are known to be dangerous.
  C making sure they have enough hot meals.
  D wearing suitable clothing for the climate.

6 What comment does Sally make about the weather during their journey?
  A Unexpected bad weather often interferes with timings for stops.
  B Whatever the weather, they will try to stick to the scheduled stop times.
  C If the weather is against them, they will be forced to abandon their trip.
  D Bad weather has less effect on motorbikes than other forms of transport.

Use of English Part 1 Multiple-choice cloze

1 Read the text below, ignoring the gaps, to find out why the 'body clock' is important.

2 For questions 1–12, read the text again and decide which answer (A, B, C or D) best fits each gap.

Example
0   B

A FUTURE IN THE DARK

For many of us, we are working, travelling and shopping in hours that used to be (0).....B........ for relaxation and sleep. But, according to the results of tests being (1).............. by scientists, we are no longer getting enough darkness in our lives. In fact, (2).............. shows that a growing number of health and environmental problems are (3).............. a loss of darkness.

Life has evolved with a day/night cycle. People who go (4).............. this day/night rhythm will notice an adverse impact on their immune systems, and that's not a good sign. We are (5).............. a conflict between what our mind wants, and what our internal body clock prepares us for. Some experts (6).............. that our biological clock is similar to the conductor of an orchestra, with the multiple rhythms of the body (7).............. the various orchestra sections.

The body clock is (8).............. on the light/dark cycle and it governs us for every (9).............. of activity and rest in our lives. It ensures that all our various internal systems are working together – this is its sole (10).............. . By moving to 24-hour living, and not taking into (11).............. the dark side, we will effectively be throwing away the advantages of evolution, (12).............. we care to admit it or not.

0 A conserved	B reserved	C upheld	D defended
1 A carried out	B carried through	C worked up	D worked off
2 A demonstration	B display	C research	D confirmation
3 A prone to	B open to	C due to	D next to
4 A down with	B without	C through	D behind
5 A creating	B contributing	C giving	D increasing
6 A explain	B discuss	C enquire	D debate
7 A describing	B corresponding	C expressing	D representing
8 A done	B based	C decided	D established
9 A prospect	B attitude	C position	D type
10 A reason	B project	C purpose	D desire
11 A interest	B importance	C detail	D account
12 A so that	B whether	C unless	D in case

Review Units 1–3

1 Correct the mistakes in adjective and adverb order.

a Tim had a rather small extremely fascinating group of friends.
b Did you at the beach enjoy yourself yesterday?
c We found the pretty restaurant easily.
d What a table disgusting oval wooden old!
e I love just your new dress.
f What a rectangular dirty enormous pencil case!
g Brenda likes quite being on her own.

2 Read definitions a–g, then write the compound nouns.

a a place where things are made or repaired
= work...............
b a problem which makes a situation worse
= set...............
c an important development in a situation
= break...............
d someone who sells papers and magazines
= news...............
e the written text of a movie
= film...............
f an unexpected result of a situation or action
= side...............
g the number of people attending an event
= turn...............

3 For questions a–c, think of one word only which can be used appropriately in all three sentences.

a What makes Jim .... out in a crowd is his long, blond hair.
We have to .... together and fight this!
Is he going to .... for election this year?
b I don't know what to .... of this strange message.
Did you .... any progress this term?
No one can .... this new machine work.
c Unfortunately, our request for a loan was .... down by the bank.
We've really .... a corner and things will improve, I'm sure.
Having .... professional, she made considerable money from athletics.

4 Put the words in the correct order beginning with the words in bold.

a photograph John I showed the.
b her for bicycle brother a bought birthday **Susie** his.
c me a fortune **My** new car cost!
d seeing Robert's insisted **The authorities** visa on.
e coffee the **Fetch** you would visitors some?
f extra the holiday students an promised day's **The** principal.
g having wisdom **My** dentist recommended teeth taken out two.
h it to careful leave appliance the switched not on after **Be** using.

5 Complete the adjectives in sentences a–e.

a Good teachers are sens............... to the needs of their students.
b After an exhaust............... international trip, the President will take a break this summer.
c Children love stories and imagin............... heroes.
d One of the most satisf............... things about sport is that it helps people develop team skills.
e Fortunately, our members of staff are all consci............... and hard-working.

6 Rewrite the second sentence in a–c keeping the meaning the same. Use three to six words including the word given.

a We think it would be better for the guests to arrive much earlier.
PREFER
We ....
the guests arrived much earlier.
b The football team managed to win the trophy for a second year.
SUCCEEDED
The football team ....
the trophy for a second year.
c Please note that our advice would be to wash the appliance before using it.
RECOMMEND
Please note that ....
the appliance before using it.

7 Complete sentences a–e using one of the nouns below.

██ upbringing   cutbacks   downfall   input   outburst

a As a member of the student union, we would very much like your .... on this matter.

b She is normally a very calm, relaxed person. I don't know where that sudden .... came from.

c The scandal surrounding the politician brought about his ....

d I regret to say that due to the .... , we will be unable to afford our annual party this year.

e What do you think has the greatest influence on your life, your .... or your education?

8 Complete sentences a–e using a suitable expression with *get*.

a These endless discussions are getting us .... It's time we reached an agreement.

b You should meet my sister. You'd get .... really well with her.

c Let's get .... to business. What's the first item on the agenda?

d As it's getting .... for 7 pm, I think we should draw the session to a close.

e We can't get .... of going to the party without offending someone.

9 Complete a–f with a relative pronoun and, where necessary, a preposition. More than one answer may be possible.

a This is the place .... the accident occurred.

b Africa, ... culture is extremely diverse, is a huge continent.

c The poet, ... very little is known, lived in the north of Scotland.

d It would be interesting to know .... Thomas decided to leave the football club.

e There was a time .... deer roamed wild through these woods.

f Debbie has painted numerous landscapes, some .... are on display in the exhibition.

10 Choose the best adjective to complete sentences 1–5.

1 The teaching staff were .... in their intention to improve examination results.
a depressed   b resolute   c curious

2 Despite the disappointing sales figures, we are .... about the future of the company.
a realistic   b curious   c optimistic

3 I now feel .... that I can make myself understood when I'm speaking Italian.
a cheerful   b depressed   c confident

4 It is hardly .... to expect to fulfil all our dreams and ambitions in life.
a realistic   b pessimistic   c optimistic

5 Everyone is .... with Sarah's moody behaviour.
a fed up   b depressed   c pessimistic

11 Use future expressions to write sentences about the likelihood of the following happening.

Example
the world's population increasing
The population of the world is bound to increase, because ...

a humans living on Mars
....

b the cost of public transport rising
....

c robots becoming part of our daily life
....

d the whole world speaking the same language
....

e your country's football team winning the world cup
....

f everyone in your class passing the exam
....

Into the wild

Reading Part 2 Gapped text

1 Read the article, and paragraphs A–G, about learning to dive, and find out what words a–c refer to.

   a double-decker bus   b swimming pool   c 'buddy'

2 Read the article again and choose from the paragraphs A–G the one which fits each gap (1–6). There is one extra paragraph which you do not need to use.

I was on holiday in the Dominican Republic with my friend when our hotel offered us a trial scuba dive. You could just put on the equipment in the swimming pool and try it for a while. My friend wasn't remotely
5 interested in getting her hair wet, let alone going scuba-diving, but it was something I'd always liked the idea of, so I gave it a go.

1 ....

Each piece looked intimidating as I put it on and I was alarmed at suddenly being in charge of the one thing
10 we can't survive without – the air we breathe. But in reality, it's no different from driving a car. You have an air gauge for your tank, which you watch as if it were the fuel supply, and a depth gauge that's like reading the speedometer. After a while, everything becomes
15 second nature.

2 ....

Suddenly, I'd discovered this completely silent world. I've been a make-up artist since I left school at 18; it's an industry where everyone is always chatting. Although there were people around during the dive,
20 the experience was entirely my own as you can't talk. I'd wanted to try a calming therapy like yoga or meditation for ages, but never got anywhere because I was always distracted by something. Here, I had to keep my breathing steady and before I knew it, I was
25 completely relaxed, lost in these beautiful colours and a myriad of sea creatures.

3 ....

I knew then that I really wanted to take up this new hobby seriously. So when I flew back to England I started an Introduction to Diving Skills course at a
30 nearby swimming pool three days later. Going from the Dominican Republic to my local pool fortunately wasn't actually as bad as I'd expected.

4 ....

I knew that your emergency air supply is actually with your dive partner, how the thing you absolutely must
35 not do is to hold your breath, because you risk bursting a lung.

And you should also swot up on where you want to go diving. For example, I really enjoyed history when I was at school, so I love wreck-diving to see it all come to life
40 and observe what I've been reading about. Diving lets you see things, in their natural surroundings, which no one has seen before.

5 ....

Our breaks away triggered my decision to teach scuba-diving. And having done the introduction course, I
45 realised how important it was to learn slowly and thoroughly – on holiday I saw people in the water who really shouldn't have been there. They didn't have a clue about the dangers of coming up too quickly, of being too long underwater, or of not watching their air.
50 I thought it would be good to learn more, to become a better diver myself and to help others dive safely.

6 ....

I teach once a month now at one of the top dive centres in the UK. It's so rewarding, especially when you come up with someone who has done their first
55 dive – they've discovered an exciting new world without boundaries – a world I love so much.

take the plunge

A It was wonderful to get so close to everything below the surface of the sea, and to spend as long as I liked just observing and moving along completely
60 weightless. It felt so effortless. I saw a turtle on that first dive, not a giant one, but at a metre from head to tail, it was big enough for me. It left me completely in awe, even though it totally ignored me.

B To become a competent diver, he recommended
65 the following steps. First, take an introductory course, which consists of five swimming pool lessons. Next, do the five theory modules, which end with a multiple-choice test. But he also pointed out that to qualify to dive with a 'buddy' of the same qualification or higher,
70 you need to complete a further four supervised dives, this time in open water.

C As well as opening up this forgotten world, it brought me into contact with my partner, Roger. I met him whilst on a training excursion – part of the course
75 – to Crystal Waters, where they've deliberately sunk a double-decker bus. I'd found the bus but wanted to go back and have another look. My friend had an ear problem so Roger, who'd been standing near us, offered to partner me. We went on countless dives
80 together and now we go on diving holidays together whenever we can.

D The very first session was extremely short but, surprisingly, it was enough time to get to grips with the three sets of equipment. There was a mask and some
85 fins, a regulator (like a snorkel mouthpiece which you breathe through) attached to a tank for the air supply, and a buoyancy control device which you had to inflate or deflate depending on how deep you wanted to dive.

E That first time you go out on your own with
90 someone who's scared and totally dependent on you, it's terrifying for you too. I used to be overly cautious – if they were even slightly worried, I took them straight back to the top. But I've learned that there are a lot of ways to help people relax underwater.

95 F That 20-minute session was followed by a dive in the sea. After that, I was hooked for good. Other than being shown how to put everything on, there was no further training; not something I'd recommend now, but at the time I was blissfully ignorant. I was taken ten
100 metres down and, despite being followed by a guide who monitored my gauges, I had the most wonderful feeling of freedom.

G The real shock came four months later when I did an open water dive at a place called Grangewaters.
105 When I went in, it only had a water temperature of about four degrees. It's full of black mud, so you can't see anything at all. By then I had done all the theory and I had a very thorough grounding in everything that could go wrong.

Vocabulary

Word formation (1)

1 Write adjective forms of these words in the correct column. You may need to change the spelling. Can you think of other adjectives with these endings? Try to add one to each column.

| | malice control force argument memory outrage possibility inform submission mystery suspicion terror advantage |

ive	ious	eous	able	ible

2 Use adjectives from 1 to replace the words in italics in sentences a–i.

a After the game, the police struggled to deal with the *scandalous* behaviour of the football supporters.

b Bella's a great friend but she does tend to be *quarrelsome* at times.

c The discovery of a *dangerous-looking* package resulted in the closure of the railway station.

d It may have been *educational* but the presentation was also extremely tedious!

e Richard is so *uncomplaining and unquestioning*. He should learn to stand up for himself more.

f Don't listen to a word Janet says – it's all *spiteful* gossip.

g William's *strange* disappearance led to a police search of the area where he lived.

h I think it would be *extremely useful* to get some work experience to help your job application.

i What is the most *unforgettable* holiday you've had? For me, it's travelling around New Zealand.

3 Look up nouns a–d below (from 1) in your dictionary and answer questions 1–3 for each one.

a submission
b argument
c memory
d terror

1 Is the verb form above or below the noun entry?
2 What other words appear to derive from the noun?
3 Can you find any new expressions or collocations?

> **tip**
> Scanning through an entry in your dictionary will help you understand word formation.

Grammar

Past tenses

1 Complete the leaflet by putting the verbs in brackets into the correct form of the present perfect or the past perfect.

Help Save The Orang-utan

Did you know that ?

- humans 1 .... (cut) down their habitat for years.

- land which 2 .... (previously/cover) with vegetation was cleared for mining and plantation.

- the orang-utan 3 .... (now/lose) 80% of its natural habitat.

- many 4 .... (kill) by farmers who believed orang-utans 5 .... (become) a pest.

- it 6 .... (recently/add) on the endangered list – only less than 50,000 now exist.

Last year a campaign was set up for people who 7 .... (never/show) active interest in conservation to help save the orang-utan.

Grammar Extra

Articles

2 Underline the correct use of the article in each pair of sentences in 1–7.

1. a Some marketing experience is desirable to run (a, no article) **business** successfully.
   b Our local cinema is back in (the, no article) **business** after its refurbishment.
2. a (The, no article) idle **gossip** can often have unexpected consequences.
   b Polly is (a, no article) **well-known** gossip, so don't tell her anything.
3. a (A, no article) previous **experience** is essential for this job.
   b The book outlines all (the, no article) **experiences** the writer had in Africa.
4. a (An, no article) **interest** in the museum's latest exhibition has been tremendous.
   b (An, no article) **interest** is payable on this account but it is so low it is not worth having.
5. a (A, The) **country** is undoubtedly a far healthier place to live than the town.
   b (A, no article) **country** which attracts many foreign visitors is Thailand.
6. a This new restaurant definitely has a touch of (the, no article) **class**.
   b (A, no article) **class** of 35 students is almost impossible to teach effectively.
7. a Due to increased security (a, no article) **people** have to put up with long delays at airports.
   b The President urged (a, the) **people** to turn out in force and vote in the referendum.

3 Complete gaps 1–12 with *a*, *an*, *the* or no article.

Every month we're giving away 1 .... magical holiday. Don't miss this unique opportunity to sample 2 .... luxury of our Transglobe holidays in one of 3 .... world's most sought-after destinations: 4 .... Pacific. Or perhaps you have a secret passion to travel to 5 .... destinations such as Venice, experience 6 .... exciting adventure in 7 .... sports car, or learn to cook 8 .... Eastern delicacies in 9 .... Orient? Just log on to our travel service website and, if you don't win, you can find 10 .... latest destinations and advice on how to plan a trip. At 11 .... end of each holiday, we'll give you 12 .... vouchers to be used towards your next holiday with us.

Listening Part 2 Sentence completion

1 Look at the photos. What athletic abilities do you think these animals have?

2 🎧 You will hear part of a radio programme about the athleticism of animals.
For questions 1–8, complete the sentences.

ANIMAL ATHLETES

One small ant can lift .... 1 times its own body weight.

Ants have an amazingly large number of .... 2.

It takes the cheetah just .... 3 seconds to cover a distance of 100m.

Cheetahs can reach high speeds, thanks to their enlarged internal organs and their .... 4.

The cheetah, however, has a low .... 5.

Springbok are frequently seen jumping in the .... 6 season.

Archer fish catch .... 7 with a 1.5 metre water jet.

The archer fish carry out their shooting in .... 8.

Use of English Part 2 Open cloze

1 Read the text about whale-watching, ignoring the gaps, and find out where the writer went and for how long.

2 For questions 1–15, read the text again and think of the word which best fits each gap.

A SUMMER AT SEA

Spending a summer in the company (0) .....**of**...... whales off the coast of Patagonia is a (1) .... in a lifetime opportunity. We spent at least twelve hours on the boat every day and learned a great (2) .... about the whales' behaviour. It seemed that our interest (3) .... reciprocated!

To encourage the whales to approach the boat we simply had to move a short distance from the coast, switch (4) .... the engines and wait. Younger whales who attempted to come closer were pushed (5) .... by their mothers, but older ones (6) .... allowed to play nearby. Some of these even came close enough for (7) .... to touch them.

On some occasions the sea seemed to be full of whales jumping (8) .... of the water but at other times we saw (9) .... any at all. Sometimes we could go for several days and (10) .... see a single whale.

Later, however, we adopted a pattern. (11) .... day we had come upon a whale and (12) .... baby and we decided to keep visiting the pair at the same time every day. At (13) .... the mother would not let the baby approach us but, as time (14) .... by, she allowed him to come closer and closer to the boat. It was a truly amazing experience to be rewarded (15) .... such trust at the end of our six weeks.

Part 4 Gapped sentences

3 Which of the words below can be used appropriately in each of sentences a–c?

■ safety   trust   faith   honesty

a Could you put your .... in him without any reservation?
b Her grandmother left her a large amount of money in .... for when she was older.
c Sometimes you can't prove someone is telling the truth – you have to take it on ....

4 Use your dictionary to look up the words <u>not</u> used in 3 and complete the idioms in a–c below. Then write an example sentence to show the meanings.

a .... in numbers
b in all ....
c lose .... in somebody

Health matters

Reading Part 3 Multiple choice

1 Read the text about human athletic abilities and find out what happened in

a 1954.

b 1968.

c 1991.

d the 1980s.

2 For questions 1–6, read the text again and choose the answer (A, B, C or D) which you think best fits according to the text.

1 What initial comment does Dr. Jack Wilmore make?
   A There will always be limits to what the human body can achieve.
   B It will become more and more difficult for athletes to break records.
   C Athletics will become one of the most popular forms of exercise.
   D Athletes will continue to surprise us with what they can achieve.

2 The writer mentions athletes like Bannister and Beamon in order to
   A demonstrate the effect their determination to win had on them.
   B prove that even their amazing achievements can be bettered.
   C exemplify what athletes can achieve under stressful conditions.
   D demonstrate how accurately we can measure what athletes are capable of.

3 Dr. Wilmore feels that attitudes within athletics are changing because
   A coaches have begun to realise the importance of more intensive training.
   B experts have begun to highlight the need for more unusual workouts.
   C athletes are now being given mental as well as physical training by experts.
   D coaches now encourage athletes to unwind between training sessions.

4 According to Dr. Wilmore, how are today's children different from years ago?
   A They participate in far more sports.
   B They begin sports at a much earlier age.
   C They become more proficient in their chosen sports.
   D They are more likely to become professional athletes.

5 Dr. Wilmore believes that women
   A have physically developed and advanced over the years.
   B perform equally well whether they are tall or short.
   C now have the same chance as boys of realising their potential.
   D are beginning to play sports at a much younger age than boys.

6 What conclusion does Dr. Wilmore make?
   A We try to push the human body to its limits at our peril.
   B We must congratulate ourselves on what athletes have achieved so far.
   C We need to do more research into what the human body is capable of.
   D We should not prejudge what might be beyond our physical capabilities.

Limits *of the* human body

In the second millennium, one frequently asked question is: What are the limits of the human body? Is there a point at which it is physically impossible to do something?

'One thing we've all learned in the last 30 years or so is that just about anything is humanly possible,' says Dr. Jack Wilmore, from Texas A&M University and author of *The Physiology of Sport and Exercise*, part of which examines the limits of the human body.

'As the new millennium progresses, I think you'll see more records continue to fall in every sport. The talent pool is better than ever. Never before have so many good athletes competed, and not just in this country, but all over the world. With more people involved and competing, records will fall and new standards will be set.'

Many believed it was physically impossible for a human to run a mile in under four minutes, but Roger Bannister proved that theory wrong with a three minute, 59 second mile (1.609 kilometres) in 1954. Today, sub four-minute miles are considered routine even in high school. And Bob Beamon stretched human performance in the 1968 Olympics with his historic long jump of 8.9027 metres. In an event in which a record is usually broken by mere inches, he shattered the previous jump by 0.6096 metres, but even his record was broken in 1991.

'We've all seen reports of people doing superhuman feats of strength under duress, such as a man lifting a car off a child,' Wilmore adds. 'So we know that the human body can do things that go far beyond normal activity. That's why it's foolish to say any record can't be broken. Who's to say it won't happen?'

One additional factor is just now becoming more understood and heavily emphasised: sports psychology. Getting inside the athlete's head can be as effective as training and long workouts.

According to Wilmore, the psychological aspect of sports should not be discounted because we now know that what makes the athlete tick mentally can be all-important. He points out that 'most professional teams have hired sports psychologists for their players. It's just another way of tapping into a human's full potential.'

'In addition, every aspect of athletics – training, nutrition, injury treatment – is far better than it's ever been. Better coaching, training techniques, equipment and other factors all contribute to make today's athlete more competitive than ever,' he believes. 'Children today tend to specialize in one or two sports instead of competing in several as was common twenty-five years ago,' Wilmore says. 'That means they start concentrating on a sport much earlier and more intensely, and they become much better at it.'

Wilmore also says that the chances of women achieving new heights in athletics could be greater than men, as more women are now involved in sports than at any other time and they are starting at about the same age as boys, meaning they are more skilled than the previous generation of girls. 'Plus, women are taller and stronger than ever. It used to be rare to see a girl who towered above you. Now it seems like you see them every day.'

'There's a lot we don't know yet about the human body,' he adds. 'And one of those things is the full range of human potential. It can be foolish to try and put limits on what the human body can do.'

Vocabulary

The body

1 Circle the word in italics to complete the expressions in a–h.

  a Could you *give* Sally *a hand/foot/arm* with sorting out the filing system tomorrow?

  b We're going out to dinner with the Browns tonight. I suppose we'll have to *hand/finger/foot the bill* as usual.

  c Initially, it can be difficult to *get* your *head/brain/mind round* advanced economics.

  d What's the name of that hotel we stayed in last year? It's *on the point/end/tip of my tongue.*

  e Bob really *put his toes/foot/ankle in it* when he moaned about his boss to Julia. She is his niece!

  f It's far too wet to go for a walk. Why don't we *shoulder/arm/head for* that café instead?

  g Rob's just got a hand-made Italian suit but it *cost an arm and a leg/hand/finger.*

  h I'm fed up with *working my fingers/hands/wrists to the bone.* It's time I found a job with shorter hours or a better salary.

2 Complete these sentences using suitable expressions from 1.

  a When we missed the bus, we decided to .... the taxi rank instead.

  b Do you remember the name of that island we visited a few years ago? It's ....

  c Jake's a bright student but he just can't seem to .... maths at all.

  d Does it really .... to fly to Australia?

  e Can anyone .... lifting these boxes? They are so heavy.

  f Just for once, can you try not to .... by saying the wrong thing to Aunty Mary?

  g I'm certainly not going to .... for you to have another free holiday with your friends!

  h I've been .... recently – I'm trying to meet a tight deadline!

Word formation (2)

3 Use your dictionary to help you fill in the nouns in the table below. More than one answer might be possible.

Verb	Noun (person)	Noun (thing)
a survive		
b perform		
c terrorise		
d coordinate		
e immigrate		
f defend		

4 Use the correct form of the words from 3 to complete sentences a–f.

  a Afternoon .... of the play begin at 2.30. Latecomers will not be admitted.

  b .... to the USA must complete all appropriate forms before entering the country.

  c The government has brought in strict new legislation to combat the threat of ....

  d Throughout her life, Maria was a strong and active .... of women's rights.

  e After the fire on the ocean-liner, ... were picked up by a passing cargo ship.

  f To be a top tennis player, you need to have excellent hand-eye ....

5 Look up *compete* in your dictionary. Scan through the words that derive from it to find:

  a words that collocate with the noun (person and thing) forms.

  b the different meanings of the adjective form.

Grammar

Direct speech

1 Read an interview with a famous explorer, Alan Bent. Then rewrite what he said into indirect speech using the verbs in brackets at the end of sentences 1–8.

Example
I met up with famous explorer Alan Bent and asked him how difficult it is to be an explorer. He said …

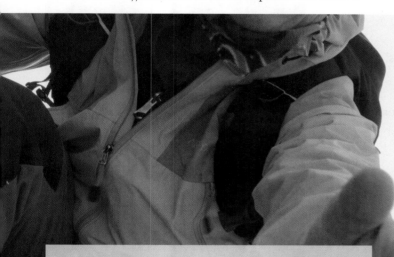

'It means I have to try to keep myself in good physical shape (1 say). Travelling to remote places means long periods away from the things most people take for granted, such as doctors (2 tell). I always wear my boots in bed (3 admit). You see, I'm very tall so my feet always stick out of the bed (4 explain). And someone in my hut was bitten by a snake once (5 add)! Oh, and I always carry an emergency medical kit, which contains a needle and thread (6 go on to say). Why don't you join me on one of these expeditions to see what it's like (7 suggest)? But make sure you keep your boots on at night (8 warn)!'

Grammar Extra

Prefixes

2 Underline the word in each group which <u>cannot</u> be used with prefixes a–g.

a **un**   reasonable/steady/productive/considerate

b **in**   natural/comprehensible/competent/credible

c **im**   mature/correct/precise/practical

d **dis**   organised/compatible/connected/honest

e **mis**   treated/understood/known/pronounced

f **non-** suitable/violent/fiction/existent

g **il**   flammable/legal/legible/logical

3 Complete sentences a–g with a word from 2.

a A .... protest against tougher laws for asylum-seekers on university fees took place in the city yesterday.

b I fear the plans for dealing with traffic congestion might turn out to be rather ....

c While most members of the staff are extremely good at their job, one or two are rather ....

d We don't have a phone any longer – the line was .... by the phone company.

e The writing on this prescription is completely .... I can't make out a single word.

f Unwanted pets can often be neglected or even .... by their owners.

g Bill has been rather .... on his feet since he fell off his bike.

Listening

Part 1 Short extracts

1 Think of five ways schools or parents can encourage children to adopt healthier lifestyles.

2 Read questions 1–6 below before you listen to the three different extracts. Then listen and choose the answer (A, B or C) which fits best.

extract one

You hear part of an interview with an actress called Mary Taylor Ward.

1 Why did Mary release her fitness video?
   A Many famous people had also done this.
   B It would help her lose weight.
   C She had a lot of relevant experience.

2 She wanted people to watch the video in order to
   A challenge their own fitness goals.
   B have a good time while exercising.
   C learn about another side of her life.

extract two

You hear part of an interview with a health expert talking about what to do at lunchtimes.

3 Why does the expert suggest a walk at lunchtimes?
   A to benefit from air and sunshine
   B to develop an appetite for lunch
   C to aid recovery from health problems

4 What does the expert advise people to do in bad weather?
   A People should read interesting magazines or books.
   B People should take part in indoor exercise.
   C People should do puzzles or something similar.

extract three

You hear two people on a radio programme talking about a recent campaign for healthy school dinners.

5 What do the speakers agree about?
   A Cafeterias are more busy.
   B Children should eat healthily.
   C Other menus should be considered.

6 The man thinks that the campaign failed because
   A the change was too sudden.
   B school cooks had to be retrained.
   C children naturally want to eat junk food.

Use of English

Part 3 Word formation

1 Read the text below quickly and decide which summary, a or b, is the most suitable.

   a A short workout is better than no workout.
   b A short workout is better than a long workout.

2 For questions 1–10, read the text again and use the words given in capitals to form a word for each gap.

a quick workout

For those with (0) .insufficient. time to spend hours working out in the gym, there is some good news. Fitness enthusiasts can (1) .... reduce their fitness workout time by two-thirds, according to recent research. Gym (2) .... has soared in recent years, much to the delight of the health and fitness industries, and doctors are hoping the (3) .... will encourage even more people to take up exercise.

The results suggest that it is not (4) .... to spend long and exhausting hours exercising when working out for a shorter time and more (5) .... achieves the same results. Participants were required to cut their exercise time, but increase the level of (6) .... of their workout. Those who exercised for the shorter time found that a significant (7) .... in body fat had occurred. Experts believe that this proves that a streamlined exercise programme is more (8) .... and also gives you more free time.

Some (9) .... point out, however, that in order to achieve goals like these, you need a good level of fitness before tackling exercise of such (10) ....

0	SUFFICIENT	6	DIFFICULT
1	EFFECT	7	REDUCE
2	MEMBER	8	BENEFIT
3	FIND	9	CRITICISE
4	PRODUCE	10	INTENSE
5	ENERGY		

Part 4 Gapped sentences

3 Think of one word only which can be used appropriately in all three sentences. The word appears in the text opposite.

The .... was challenging for even the brighter students.

Without regular .... we put on weight much more easily.

When I was learning to play the piano I had to repeat the same .... again and again.

4 Which of these words below can be used appropriately in all three sentences (a–c)?

    news   novel   story   tale

   a The .... is about a young man who travels round the USA.
   b Wait until you've heard both sides of the .... before you make a judgement.
   c Today's front page .... concerns revelations about the travel industry.

5 Look up the words <u>not</u> used in 4 in your dictionary. Write sentences to show at least two different meanings or uses of the words.

Would you believe it?

Reading

Part 4 Multiple matching

1 Read the text about superheroes. How does the writer ultimately feel about the characters in the films?

- inspired
- disappointed
- angry

2 In which section (A–F) of the text are 1–12 mentioned?

an assault on an innocent person	1 …	2 …
a seemingly endless collection of costumes	3 …	
a box-office hit for superheroes	4 …	
a heroine frightened of beginning relationships with men	5 …	
a summary of the drawbacks of being a superhero	6 …	7 …
a secret and harmful invention that is uncovered	8 …	
a heroine who seems to detest herself	9 …	
an expert that advises and guides a heroine	10 …	11 …
a search for something which causes global suffering	12 …	

CAN GIRLS BE SUPERHEROES?

A

Batman has flapped to the top of the charts, with $200m in his vault. Superman has put in yet another appearance; to those who inhabit out-of-town multiplexes, it is easy to believe that we are being held
5 hostage by larger-than-life male superheroes. If little boys have the bat and the alien that wears turquoise tights, who can little girls admire? I have a few hours to spare one night after work, so I head off in search of an inspirational female superhero at the DVD shop and
10 take out four films: *Catwoman*, *Elektra*, *Lara Croft Tomb Raider: The Cradle of Life* and *Charlie's Angels: Full Throttle*. They will have a heroine to send Batman back to his cave for me, won't they?

B

My first supergirl is Catwoman. Patience Philips, played
15 by Halle Berry, is a graphic designer at a cosmetics
company. When Patience discovers that evil genius
Laurel Hedare has designed a new face cream that will
make all Americans ugly, Hedare ensures that she
meets with a fatal accident. Although Patience dies, she
20 is reanimated by cats. She finds a guru who says,
'Catwomen are not contained by the rules of society.
You will often be lonely and misunderstood.' I begin to
despair. Catwoman, I decide, is a loser. She finds a cop
boyfriend and looks up at him adoringly. She steals a
25 shopful of jewellery and returns it in a paper bag
marked: 'Sorry'. Doesn't being a supergirl mean never
having to say you're sorry? She is also thick. Hedare
frames her for murder – easily. Kitty has to sob (to a
man!) to be released from jail. My finger trembles over
30 'Eject' but relents. Perhaps she'll improve. She doesn't.
Although she does succeed in rescuing the world from
killer face-cream, as the credits roll the boyfriend is
dumped and Patience pads into the moonlight alone.
This is not superheroic, it's a pathetic example of
35 unnecessary self-sacrifice.

C

My next potential idol is Elektra, from the 'supergirl'
class. Elektra is a reincarnated, knife-throwing, ninja
babe-assassin who can only stab people if she is
wearing a red satin bustier. 'Legend tells of a warrior
40 – a lost soul,' says a disembodied voice on the film. A
pattern is emerging here – a superheroine always has
to be lost; she gets good thighs but is denied street
maps. 'It is her destiny to tip the balance of good and
evil.' Elektra is not only lost, she is, according to mentor
45 Terence Stamp, 'poisoned by tragedy.' Even her
protector cannot protect her
from the truth. My heart
sinks. Elektra has an
obsessive compulsive
50 disorder and likes to
arrange bananas and
shampoo into rows.
She's bitter – 'Nobody
tells the truth about
55 themselves' – and her
dialogue is culled from
television scripts – 'My
mother died when I was
young. I should go. Thanks for
60 dinner.' Like Catwoman,
Elektra is not super enough
to have a functioning
relationship. When she
does kiss a man, she
65 panics. 'I'm not the kind of person you
should get involved with,' she sobs.

D

Another pattern seems to be emerging. At one point,
the villainous Hand breathes on Elektra's face and gives
her spots. In Superland, the worse thing you can do to
70 a superwoman (after making her a superwoman) is to
give her acne. Elektra triumphs over Hand but, like the
Cat, she pays the price and takes the fall. Just two films
in, the message to women from Hollywood is: You
want to be a superwoman? Are you sure? Well,
75 unhappiness is mandatory and being miserable, vital.
This is the sad reality of what you will have to endure
as a heroine. Elektra clearly does not like it and slumps
into a puddle of self-loathing. She stares at a ninja girl
of thirteen and whines: 'Please don't let her turn out
80 like me.'

E

The girls with supernatural powers were unsuper. So I
turn to the girls with superskills, beginning with Lara
Croft, as played by Angelina Jolie in *Lara Croft Tomb
Raider: The Cradle of Life.* Lara is like the girls I was at
85 school with: an ordinary suburban girl who talks like a
film actress and lives in a large house in the
countryside. Her quest is to find the mythical Pandora's
Box, the source of the world's grief, before evil scientists
get hold of it. She drives a motorbike along the Great
90 Wall of China and sky-dives off a bank, but then 'The
Message' pops up again. 'You're afraid of letting anyone
in,' says her boyfriend. Lara shoots him, without any
apparent justification, then strikes the pose of a noble
superheroine-in-solitude. Do you understand, ladies?
95 Superwoman can't have a super relationship or super
contentment and the pay-off for her super gift is
isolation, loneliness, misanthropy and, eventually, no
doubt, contracting some ghastly disease in her old age.

F

My quest for a superwoman ends with *Charlie's
100 Angels: Full Throttle.* In scene one, the Angels,
wearing very tight clothes, get rid of a gaggle of
cheery gangsters. They return to LA, to serve their
patriarch Charlie – an elusive man who delivers their
orders, assists from afar, and congratulates them at
105 appropriate moments – and are informed they
have to recover some important data for
the FBI. I watch as they succeed with a
combination of looking gorgeous, karate,
and disco-dancing. They change their outfits
110 practically every thirty
seconds and wear aquamarine
mascara and, after two hours, the
Angels see off baddie Demi Moore.
It is certainly not heroic. My TV screams for
115 mercy. My girls-night-out in Superland is over.
Under their masks, I saw only weakness.
Batman has won.

Vocabulary

Truth and lies

1 Choose the best answer (A, B or C) to complete
sentences 1–5.

   1 The accused tried in vain to .... the true
      nature of the crime he had committed.
      A conceal   B shelter   C protect
   2 We have evidence to prove that the new car was
      paid for with .... money.
      A copy   B counterfeit   C mock
   3 We have complete .... in the
      government's ability to solve problems of
      unemployment.
      A loyalty   B honour   C faith
   4 Stuart managed to .... everyone in with
      elaborate stories about his childhood.
      A have   B put   C take
   5 You can rely on Elizabeth to give you good
      advice. I'd .... her judgement every time.
      A trust   B presume   C assume

Words with similar meanings (2)

2 Look up the words in 1–3 in your dictionary.
Match one from each pair with definition a, then
complete the definitions for b.

   1 snigger/giggle
      a laugh in a silly way when amused,
         embarrassed or nervous
      b laugh in a(n) .... way
   2 whisper/mumble
      a speak in a quiet way that is not clear
      b deliberately speak very quietly so ....
   3 eavesdrop/overhear
      a hear, especially by accident, a conversation in
         which you are not involved
      b .... to what other people are saying

3 Complete sentences a–c with words from 2 in the
correct form.

   a How do you know that? You must have been
      .... We haven't told anyone!
   b All the students .... nervously as they
      waited for their exam results.
   c Try not to .... when you speak. No one
      can hear you properly.

Meanings of *hold*

4 How many different meanings and uses of *hold*
can you think of? Compare your ideas with your
dictionary. Which meanings and uses did you not
think of?

5 Complete sentences a–f with a suitable word or
phrase (1–6).

     1 for questioning
     2 responsible
     3 a party
     4 extreme views
     5 my attention
     6 the line

   a Teachers will be *held* .... for the behaviour
      of pupils in their class.
   b Two men were *held* .... in connection
      with the break-ins.
   c I enjoyed the play but it didn't *hold* .... as
      much as the playwright's last one.
   d The election result was surprising as the winning
      candidate *held* ....
   e We're going to *hold* .... next month for
      our anniversary.
   f Can you *hold* .... and I'll put you through
      to my secretary?

6 Match the different meanings of *hold* from 5 with
definitions a–f below.

   a wait momentarily
   b make liable
   c have an event
   d kept somewhere and not allowed to leave
   e possess or show
   f keep someone's interest

Grammar

Modals

1 Circle the most suitable modal in these sentences.

a You *shouldn't/mustn't* have wasted your time typing out the letter. You knew we weren't going to send it.

b A work permit *must/need* be obtained in advance by anyone intending to live and reside in the country.

c You *need/should* always seek advice before signing any legal documentation.

d The staff *must/should* be very contented working here. Everyone has a smile on their face.

e I suppose your order *might/can* have been lost. These things can happen.

f I'm afraid I *can't/shouldn't* make out what the writing on this prescription says – it's illegible.

g You *ought to/need* think carefully before making any decision.

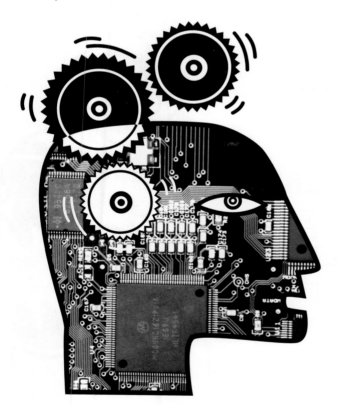

2 Complete these sentences using modals of assumption or deduction and the correct form of one of the verbs below.

◼ miss   delay   receive   be   pass   do

a She <u>must have passed</u> the exam – look, she's smiling and laughing!

b The hotel .... our booking as they had no reservation under the name 'Wright'.

c It's odd that James hasn't arrived yet – do you think his plane .... ?

d I think you .... him actually, he's normally gone by this time.

e You .... well at the interview, otherwise they wouldn't have offered you the job!

f Surely Sally .... serious when she said she was going to sell all her possessions and go and live on a desert island?

3 Match the modals in a–c with meanings 1–3.

a Visitors needn't return the museum catalogue – it's theirs to keep.

b Passengers with season tickets don't need to purchase tickets on a daily basis.

c I needn't have called directory enquiries. I had the number in my diary after all.

1 It was done, but it was not necessary.
2 It is not necessary, but can be done (if required).
3 This is not necessary.

4 Complete sentences a–d with *needn't* or *needn't have* and the correct form of the verbs in brackets.

a 'I stayed up late revising, but when I saw the exam paper, I realised I .... (worry)!'

b 'You .... (pay) anything now. A bill will be sent to you in due course.'

c 'Apparently fans .... (arrive) early for the concert – there will be plenty of available seats.'

d 'We .... (spend) all that time looking for a bank – there was a cash machine here!'

Listening

Part 4 Multiple matching

1 Do you agree with these comments about food?

- Breakfast is the most important meal of the day.
- Eating carrots helps you see in the dark.
- Eating fish will make you more clever.

2 🎧 Listen to five people talking about popular beliefs connected with food and complete the exam task below.

For 1–5, choose from the list A–H the person who is speaking.

A a teacher

B a nutritionist

C an athlete

D a mother

E a chef

F a doctor's receptionist

G a researcher

H a writer

Speaker 1 [ ] [1]

Speaker 2 [ ] [2]

Speaker 3 [ ] [3]

Speaker 4 [ ] [4]

Speaker 5 [ ] [5]

For 6–10, choose from the list A–H each speaker's beliefs about a particular food.

A It improves your mental abilities.

B It can cut visits to the doctor.

C It leads to poorer performance if missed.

D It will make you beautiful.

E It can develop physical strength.

F It helps improve one of the senses.

G It is normally avoided if you have a temperature.

H It keeps you young.

Speaker 1 [ ] [6]

Speaker 2 [ ] [7]

Speaker 3 [ ] [8]

Speaker 4 [ ] [9]

Speaker 5 [ ] [10]

Use of English

Part 1 Multiple-choice cloze

1 Read the newspaper article below about a problem with the lack of sunlight in an Italian village. What is the possible solution?

2 Read the article again and complete gaps 1–12 with the best option (A, B, C or D).

Brilliant idea to light up village

A village (0) ......B......... the foothills of the Italian Alps that sees no sun for nearly three months a year is to (1) .... its winters by using a giant mirror to reflect sunshine onto its (2) .... square.

This week, the 197 inhabitants of Viganella, which is buried in the (3) .... Antrona valley, north of Turin, will gather for the arrival of a tailor-made (4) .... of steel 8m wide and 5m high. It will be flown by helicopter to a (5) .... spot on the mountainside.

The mayor, Pierfranco Midali, who is spearheading the project, is (6) .... that the hamlet will no longer have to suffer from the (7) .... absence of direct sunlight for 83 days a year, from November 11 to February 2.

Midali first set the ball rolling with a (8) .... he made seven years ago, after he commissioned a sundial for the façade of the parish church. He told the architect who made this that if he could (9) .... of a solution to bring the sun to Viganella, he would (10) .... it all the way.

Weighing more than a ton, and (11) .... on the nearby Colna Peak, the mirror will reflect the sun's rays onto the village square half a mile away and light up an area of 30 square metres for at least six hours a day. The mirror's maker has (12) .... it will stand up to the strongest winds and will last at least 30 years.

0	A	at	B	in	C	under	D around
1	A	enlighten	B	reduce	C	brighten	D lift
2	A	first	B	main	C	important	D open
3	A	narrow	B	thin	C	shallow	D brief
4	A	material	B	blanket	C	cover	D sheet
5	A	concluded	B	designated	C	best	D specialised
6	A	confident	B	ensured	C	convincing	D ascertaining
7	A	full	B	intact	C	complete	D whole
8	A	word	B	comment	C	saying	D speech
9	A	draw	B	decide	C	make	D think
10	A	hold	B	carry	C	support	D stand
11	A	held	B	positioned	C	lain	D dropped
12	A	insured	B	thought	C	guaranteed	D hoped

Review Units 4–6

1 Replace the words in italics with a suitable expression containing one of these words.

▪ hand head tongue fingers foot

a I *offended someone unintentionally* when I criticised the picture. I didn't realise Sue had painted it.

b I'm starving. Let's *go to* the nearest restaurant.

c Can anyone *help me* to carry these books to the library?

d There must be more to life than *working hard or for long hours* every day.

e What was that film we saw last week? *I can't remember at the moment.*

2 Correct the six mistakes with past tenses in this paragraph.

Example
University students ~~had have~~ made it their mission to save the Iberian lynx from extinction by undertaking a sponsored walk.

The students have become aware of the plight of the lynx when they had been starting some research into various species as part of their course. It has appeared that the lynx had being threatened by several factors. In recent years, their numbers were been depleted and their natural habitat has decreasing.

3 Choose the best word to complete a–f.

a Police have discovered that *counterfeit/copy* money was used to pay for the goods.

b Remember that whenever you need help, you can *count/calculate* on me.

c I have to confess that I deliberately *overheard/eavesdropped on* an extremely interesting conversation yesterday.

d The con man managed to *take/put* us in with his lies.

e What are you two *whispering/mumbling* about? What's the big secret?

f Kate could be an excellent student but spends too much time *sniggering/giggling* at silly jokes.

4 For questions a–c, think of one word only which can be used appropriately in all three sentences.

a You can .... on me for support in the meeting.
Children learn to .... at quite a young age.
I completely agree with you but my opinion doesn't really ....

b He .... that it was getting even colder in the evenings.
I always .... the school rules when I was a pupil.
The scientists .... the behaviour of rats during the experiment.

c A general election will be .... next month.
Three men have been .... for questioning about the robbery.
Visitors are .... responsible for any damage caused.

5 Correct any incorrect negative prefixes in a–i.

a insteady ....
b unviolent ....
c unfortunate ....
d inprecise ....
e illegal ....
f innatural ....
g misorganised ....
h non-understood ....
i dispronounced ....

6 Read the text below and correct the four mistakes with modals.

Jane Henley would not be happier after winning in the international track and field event at the age of 19. Her parents might have been delighted with her success. It mustn't have been easy making the sacrifices necessary for their daughter to realise her dream. They admitted they were very nervous, however, they needn't have worry!

7 Complete the dialogues using *a, an, the* or no article.

1 A: Do you ever travel to work by .... train?
  B: Never – I prefer to go by .... bus or on .... foot.

2 A: What can .... governments do to help .... unemployed?
  B: They can increase .... unemployment benefits for .... start.

3 A: What do you think is .... main difference between .... British and .... French?
  B: Probably .... food they eat!

4 A: Were you at .... work when you heard .... news about the earthquake?
  B: I was at .... home watching TV.

5 A: I'll pick you up after .... dinner and we'll go to .... cinema.
  B: Fine – we'll have finished .... meal by about 7.30.

6 A: What does Jim want to do when he leaves .... school?
  B: He wants to join .... police force.

7 A: Do you have .... favourite flower?
  B: Yes – it's .... orchid.

8 A: What do you consider to be .... greatest invention ever?
  B: .... computer, of course.

8 Complete the adjectives below, then use these adjectives in sentences a–e.

▓ suspic..............   inform..............
  court..............   malic..............
  outrag..............

a David is extremely charming. I've never met anyone so .... and polite.
b If you're confused about technology, read this book. It's .... and really useful.
c The candidate failed to win due to the .... rumours the opposition had spread.
d What's that man doing? He's behaving in a very .... manner.
e She's one of the world's most .... singers and always causes controversy.

9 Rewrite this dialogue in indirect speech using the correct form of the reporting verbs in a–f. More than one answer may be possible.

Example
TED: What motivated you to become a safari guide?
<u>Ted asked Sarah what had motivated her</u>
<u>to become a safari guide.</u> .... (ask)

SARAH: Ever since I was a child, I've been desperate to travel.
a .... (admit)

Have you ever been on safari?
b .... (ask)

TED: No, I haven't.
c .... (tell)

But it is one of my ambitions.
d .... (add)

SARAH: I hope one day you will go on one.
e .... (go on to say)

Why don't you take a place on my next trip?
f .... (offer)

10 Rewrite the second sentence in a–c keeping the meaning the same. Use between three to six words including the word given.

a Bill said, 'I'll take you to the airport in my car'.
  GIVE
  Bill ....
  a lift to the airport.

b Everyone believed my neighbour's claims about once being a famous singer.
  TAKEN
  Everyone ....
  my neighbour's claims about once being a famous singer.

c What did you think about the exam? I couldn't understand the last question at all.
  HEAD
  What did you think about the exam? I couldn't
  ....
  the last question.

Traces of the past

Reading

Part 1 Themed texts

1 Read the three extracts opposite quickly and match headings a–c with the most suitable extract.

   a Step back into time
   b Remembering a tragedy
   c A past beauty of many faces

2 For questions 1–6, read the extracts again and choose the answer (A, B, C or D) which you think fits best.

extract one

She was the Queen of the Deep South. An aristocratic party girl decked in jewels. She could be charming and romantic. She could be corrupt and racist. But most of all she had jazz rhythms beating in her carefree heart. Perhaps this was why she was called 'the city that care forgot'. But 05 in 2005 New Orleans was submerged in the flood waters of a hurricane called Katrina. Beneath the murky waters lay a city it was hoped would one day be drained, salvaged and built again but which had, for a brief spell, been 10 robbed of its unique heritage, architecture and spirit. Today she is rising again from the devastation caused by the floods. Her inhabitants have returned, jazz fills the streets again and the tourists are back, even though her restoration 15 still has a long way to go. One of the questions on people's minds is: 'When she returns to full glory, will the Queen of the Deep South's personality have changed?'

We shall have to wait and see but, for many, New Orleans remains a city loved for its diversity and its tolerance, for 20 its chicory-flavoured sweet, dark coffee, and its broad, slow-paced southern drawl. It always maintained its sense of nobility, high-minded civility and air of historic superiority and is undoubtedly remembered as such by millions of tourists. Despite being a town of great luxury and 25 privilege, it was also something of a paradox. Beneath its façade of gentility, its hands were as dirty as the rich deep mud of the Mississippi. Corruption and racism stood alongside great poverty, high crime and unemployment in many of its 30 African-American slums.

Text based on 'Is this the death of the big easy?', Peter Sheridan, *The Daily Express*, 2005.

1 What comments does the writer make about restoring New Orleans?
  A Many people are questioning how long this will take.
  B It is unsure whether she will have the same character.
  C Inhabitants believe the damage adds to her heritage.
  D Tourists are keen to witness the process of restoration.

2 What is one of the contrasts associated with the city?
  A A much darker side was concealed behind the charm.
  B The people's apparent happiness covered up desperation.
  C Wealthy tourists were never aware of its poverty.
  D Its buildings appeared strong but were built on weak foundations.

extract two

Genesis Fine Limited Editions in association with the *Mary Rose Trust* is proud to announce the re-publication [35] of a charming piece of nineteenth-century literature – a beautifully bound book detailing the sinking of the famous Tudor warship. [40]

On 19th July 1545, the *Mary Rose* – second largest ship of Henry VIII's mighty fleet – set sail from Spithead to challenge the French [45] invaders. In full view of the King and his assembled forces, the great ship keeled and then capsized. She sank rapidly to the bottom of [50] the Solent taking with her almost 700 men. She stayed there until she was successfully raised four centuries later in 1982.

The Relic of the Mary Rose was first published in 1842. It contains an eye-witness account of the [55] tragedy by Sir Peter Carew, a near relation of the ill-fated captain, and an up-to-the-minute report of a Victorian attempt to raise the wreck.

This exquisite miniature volume is now available again: as a strictly limited edition of 750 copies, [60] each numbered and signed by Margaret Rule, Archaeological Director of the *Mary Rose Trust*, who has written a new foreword. The binding of the book is in full leather with gilt decoration and an inlay of beautifully polished and lacquered [65] fine English oak from the *Mary Rose*. A donation in respect of each copy sold will be made towards the Trust's vital restoration fund; for, in a very real sense, the Trust's work has only just begun. [70]

extract three

Your visit to the Bay of Naples should, without doubt, include a visit to **Herculaneum** which was destroyed by Vesuvius in AD79. The site is much smaller than Pompeii, mainly because of the fact that it was a smaller town. It still lies beneath the modern suburb of Ercolano. It's [75] a pity that so little has been excavated but progress is limited because the area's largest second-hand clothing market sits on top of it. Make sure you check this out too!

And if you've already been to Pompeii, you're going to be even more impressed with Herculaneum because it [80] has buildings that are generally better preserved than Pompeii. Some still have upper storeys and some even have original furniture from 2000 years ago. Boathouses, baths, opulent villas and gardens show what a beautiful place this must have been in Roman times. There is even [85] a wine shop with the counter and all the containers still in place – it's astonishing!

The easiest way to get to Herculaneum is via the local railway. Take the Circumvesuviana railway and get out at Ercolano Scavi station, then walk 1 km down the hill. At [90] the entrance to the archaeological park, pick up a map showing the gridlike layout of the dig. Splash out on an audio guide (€6 for one, €9 for two: you'll need to leave an ID card) and head down the tunnel to start the tour at the shoreline. Prepare to be amazed! [95]

---

3 The disaster of the *Mary Rose* occurred
  A on her return from war with the French.
  B during her first voyage.
  C despite warnings from the captain.
  D while the King was watching.

4 The republished book features
  A an account of the building of the *Mary Rose*.
  B a description of the moment she sank.
  C information about the *Mary Rose Trust*.
  D different reactions to the disaster.

5 Herculaneum is difficult to excavate because of
  A the possibility of producing further eruptions.
  B the depth and position it is buried at.
  C the disturbance it would cause to existing buildings and facilities.
  D the potential theft of any items uncovered.

6 What surprised the writer about Herculaneum?
  A The low number of visitors.
  B Visiting the site on foot was difficult.
  C There is an unusual route into the city.
  D Many items have remained intact.

Vocabulary

Phrasal verbs with *off* and *in*

1 Complete 1–5 with phrasal verbs formed from these verbs plus *off*.

| take   bring   call   cut   show |

1 During winter, the mountain villages are often .... by heavy snowstorms.
2 No-one expected Colin to organise the end-of-term party by himself, but he managed to .... it ....
3 Ted thinks he knows everything – he's always .... his expertise in something or other.
4 Plans for the wedding were unfortunately .... at the last minute as the bride fell in love with the best man.
5 Peterson's career really .... following the huge box-office hit of his first feature film.

2 Match the phrasal verbs from 1 with meanings a–e.

a end suddenly and unexpectedly
b succeed against expectations
c begin to be successful
d to be isolated
e try to impress people

3 Use the correct form of the verbs from 1 with the particle *in* to complete dialogues 1–5 below.

1 A: That's terrible – you must feel absolutely awful!
  B: I just can't believe it. I had to read his letter again and again to ....
2 A: Are you ready to talk to the candidates?
  B: Yes. Will you please .... them .... now?
3 A: Why were the police .... ?
  B: To investigate allegations of bribery and corruption.
4 A: More should be done to help one-parent families.
  B: But the government has only recently .... new measures to help them.
5 A: Have you met Andy's cousin? He's very rude.
  B: You can say that again. He always .... whenever someone tries to speak.

4 Match the phrasal verbs from 3 with meanings a–e.

a introduce
b bring here
c try to understand the meaning
d interrupt
e request to come and help

5 Choose the correct particle in sentences a–e to make a two-part phrasal verb.

a If you are told *in/off*, you have upset someone by doing something wrong or badly.
b If you take someone *in/off*, you let them stay at your house.
c If you go *in/off* something, you don't like it anymore.
d If you keep something *in/off*, you prevent yourself from saying what you think.
e If something pulls people *in/off*, it makes a lot of people want to see it.

Grammar
Participle clauses

1 Complete the encyclopedia entry below using the correct participle form of the verbs in brackets.

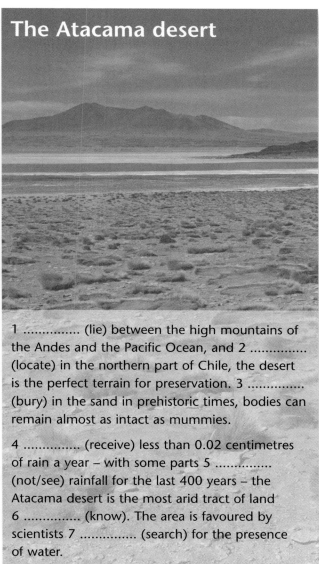

The Atacama desert

1 .... (lie) between the high mountains of the Andes and the Pacific Ocean, and 2 .... (locate) in the northern part of Chile, the desert is the perfect terrain for preservation. 3 .... (bury) in the sand in prehistoric times, bodies can remain almost as intact as mummies.

4 .... (receive) less than 0.02 centimetres of rain a year – with some parts 5 .... (not/see) rainfall for the last 400 years – the Atacama desert is the most arid tract of land 6 .... (know). The area is favoured by scientists 7 .... (search) for the presence of water.

Grammar Extra
Suffixes

2 Match groups a–h with a suitable suffix. Remember you may have to change the spelling.

    ess   hood   ship   ness   ist   less   ese   ful   ee

a train/employ/attend
b friend/relation/owner
c steward/act/host
d child/neighbour/likely
e happy/like/sweet
f special/capital/art
g care/hope/rest
h China/Portugal/Lebanon

3 Which group from 2 can take two suffixes?

4 Complete sentences a–l with the words in brackets and one of the suffixes below.

    ian   cy   ment   ty

a (politics) Only one .... decided to back the revaluation of the currency yesterday.
b (content) They say that the secret of .... lies in leading a simple life.
c (anxious) The selection process caused great .... in applicants for the job.
d (music) Even a talented .... can have problems finding work.
e (clear) One of the most important qualities of effective writing is ....
f (fulfil) Vocational jobs such as teaching can bring great ....
g (democratic) .... means government by the people for the people.
h (argue) It is often difficult to make up after a heated ....
i (technical) Unfortunately the .... was unable to repair the computer.
j (secret) Each committee member must be sworn to .... prior to the ceremony.
k (authentic) Experts consider the .... of the manuscript to be under serious doubt.
l (diplomatic) Tact and .... are skills that are not easily learned.

The big issues

Reading Part 3 Multiple choice

1 Read the text about a new computer program and find out what it aims to do. Is it successful?

WE'RE FUNNY IN THE BRAIN

A computer walks into a bar … no, hang on, why did the mainframe computer cross the road? Please, don't groan. Information Technology (IT) humour doesn't work very well. Computers don't do jokes and the people who
5 understand computers aren't famous for being a load of laughs either. But Dr Binsted, an expert in Artificial Intelligence (AI), plans to change that. If her project succeeds, your computer of the future could be swapping puns (jokes on word play) and wisecracks with you faster
10 than a New York cab driver.

Binsted is one of the speakers on humour, art and the brain, at the Festival of Art and the Mind, in England. She will unveil a computer program called 'WISCRAIC' (Witty Idiomatic Sentence Creation Revealing Ambiguity in
15 Context) which will entertain the audience with its stock of clever jokes. However, since examples include 'The book thief was caught read-handed instead of 'red-handed', it's obvious that Binsted's cyber comedian cannot be relied upon for its ability to make people laugh.
20 But that is one reason why the project is so interesting. The fact that *Wiscraic* and his punning companion *Jape* (Joke Analysis Production Engine) find even basic humour so hard, despite access to vast language databases, is a vivid demonstration of what a difficult thing humour is.

25 They are certainly nowhere near answering the most fundamental question – why do human beings laugh and make jokes at all? Why is it that whenever two or three people are gathered together, we smile and send out a series of short noises, each about 75 milliseconds long,
30 repeated at regular intervals? One rather surprising answer is social dominance.

When researcher Professor Provine, at the University of Maryland, eavesdropped in clubs and bars to find exactly what happens when people laugh, he discovered that it is
35 something women do in response to men. When talking to men, women will laugh 127 per cent more than their male audience, while men talking to a female audience will laugh seven per cent less than their audience. 'Laughter, like many other social activities, is connected with status
40 and the desire of the male to impress,' Provine says. 'Top people don't laugh; you laugh at what they say.' Both male and female listeners laugh more when a man is speaking, but in neither case do the jokes have to be any good.

But when we laugh at something that is funny, what goes
45 on in our brains? Understanding this is the ultimate dream of neuroscience because while we can locate memories, speech and even religious experiences in the brain, jokes turn out to be even more complex. Neuroscientists have known for some years that if you damage the right side of
50 your brain, story-telling jokes of the 'Man walks into a bar' variety are lost on you – but comedy based on clumsy actions or embarrassing situations is guaranteed a laugh. When subjects were recently put in a scanner at the Institute of Neurology in London and told a popular joke,
55 an area at the back of their frontal lobes was activated. But a rather different picture emerged when researchers at the institute told subjects puns or what they called 'semantic jokes' – 'Why don't sharks bite lawyers?' 'Professional courtesy.' While both types amused the part
60 of the brain which deals with reward and control, they arrived there via different routes. The puns went through an area that controls speech (the Broca's), while the 'semantic' jokes went through the temporal lobes.

So it's obvious that humour is, in fact, a serious matter,
65 with a strong social dimension that needs a surprising amount of brain power and a willingness to break rules. Attempting to programme these requirements into a computer sounds unrealistic at best. 'It's true that in science fiction robots can usually do everything – except
70 make jokes,' Binsted says, 'but one of the aims of AI is

to model what humans do and to replicate it.' She defends *Wiscraic's* playground jokes with an analogy about computer-composed music. 'It goes all the way from the sophisticated music of Beethoven down to short, simple tunes in adverts and right now we are still at the advertising end! But it's a start. If computers are going to interact with humans via language, they are going to have to do humour.' What's intriguing is just how unsuccessful the computer is – 'The friendly gardener had thyme (a garden herb, as opposed to time) for the women' – compared with the real thing, like Groucho Marx's 'I have had a perfectly wonderful evening. But this wasn't it.' Why exactly one works perfectly and the others make everyone groan is the kind of question that keeps academics in work for decades.

But already Binsted's joking computer has its fans in at least one place where language is highly valued. It is currently being used to teach English to Japanese

90 students who can chat with a screen. The program makes a joke like the 'friendly gardener' one and then deconstructs it to explain the idiomatic use of the word *time*. 'We've found that students remember more and keep working longer when the screen throws up the 95 occasional joke,' Binsted says.

2 For questions 1–6, read the text again and choose the correct answer (A, B, C or D) which you think fits best.

1 What statement does the writer make in the first paragraph?
   A There are numerous jokes about the computer industry.
   B IT people often make up amusing jokes about computers.
   C Some computers are capable of making up their own jokes.
   D The IT industry is not well-known for its sense of humour.

2 According to the writer, the computer program called *Wiscraic*
   A has been programmed to understand the real meaning of humour.
   B has a long way to go before it succeeds in its comic aims.
   C would greatly benefit from more access to language databases.
   D is capable of making large numbers of people laugh hysterically.

3 One explanation for why humans laugh in certain situations is that it
   A helps them demonstrate their position in society.
   B provides a welcome change of pace in conversations.
   C enables people to establish closer contact with one another.
   D is a means of showing appreciation of what we find funny.

4 Scientists have only recently discovered that
   A damage to the right brain can interfere with our understanding of jokes.
   B people find puns and semantic jokes more appealing than ordinary jokes.
   C the brain processes different kinds of jokes in different ways.
   D programming a computer to process jokes like humans would be impossible.

5 Binsted compares *Wiscraic* to computer-composed music in order to
   A prove how capable the computerised humour program is.
   B show how computerised humour is still in its infancy.
   C illustrate the skills needed by humans to match computerised humour.
   D highlight the number of academics involved in the humour project.

6 What happened when *Wiscraic* was used as a tool for teaching English to Japanese students?
   A It caused minor problems for some of the students.
   B The students understood the jokes immediately.
   C A teacher had to be present to explain the jokes.
   D The jokes helped the students become more effective in their studies.

Vocabulary

Compound adjectives

1 Match groups a–e with 1–5 to make compound adjectives. Then use your dictionary to find four more compound adjectives beginning with *self*.

a	half-/light-/broken-	1	minded
b	open-/narrow-/broad-	2	made
c	full-/part-/first-	3	handed
d	left-/right-/single-	4	hearted
e	man-/hand-/self-	5	time

2 Use compound adjectives from 1 to complete sentences a–e. More than one answer may be possible.

a Due to current expansion, there are vacancies for two .... members of staff.

b These scissors are specially designed to be used by .... people.

c The new play at the Criterion theatre is a .... look at life in suburbia.

d He's so .... – he's not prepared to listen to anyone else's opinion.

e Have you seen these necklaces? They are all .... in Chile!

Negative adjectives

3 Write the opposites of words a–h using a <u>negative</u> prefix.

a penetrable   impenetrable

b tolerable   ....

c perceptible   ....

d reversible   ....

e sensitive   ....

f stable   ....

g measurable   ....

h sociable   ....

4 Match the <u>opposites</u> from 3 with the similar meanings in 1–8 below. Check any words you are not sure of in your dictionary.

1	uncaring	5	indistinguishable
2	incalculable	6	unbearable
3	insecure	7	inaccessible
4	inhospitable	8	unchangeable

5 Complete sentences a–h with a suitable adjective from exercises 3 or 4. More than one answer may be possible.

a Which of these paintings is the original? They're completely .... to me.

b They're quite an .... family. They never really go out and mix with anyone.

c The heat is .... in here. I can't believe the air conditioning is still broken.

d Due to torrential weather conditions the mountain pass is .... via this route.

e My little sister is still quite .... and always seems to feel self-conscious.

f There are very few decisions in life that are .... in my experience.

g Torrel's work is known throughout the world – his contribution to the arts is ....

h I don't want to sound .... but it's time you sorted out your own mistakes!

Grammar
Conditionals

1 Look at the picture of the man and complete sentences a–e with a suitable conditional phrase using the verb in brackets.

Example

<u>He would not have slipped</u> (slip) if he hadn't gone so close to the edge.

a If he shouts for help, no one .... (hear) him.

b If he .... (take) a photo, he wouldn't be in trouble!

c If he could reach his mobile, he .... (call) for help.

d If he .... (reach) the tree, he could climb to safety.

e If he had told someone where he was, they .... (find) him.

2 Rewrite these conditional sentences using the prompts given.

a My aunt lent me the money, so I was able to go abroad.
If my aunt ....

b Never stay out in the midday sun because of the risk of getting burned.
If you ....

c Thomas had three jobs over the summer and then he was able to buy a motorbike.
If Thomas ....

d It's not certain that I can offer you a scholarship, but I'd like to know how you feel about it.
If I were ....

e Profits are down because demand for our products is falling.
If demand ....

3 Complete these conditional sentences using the correct form of the verb in brackets.

a When petrol .... (ignite), it .... (go up) in flames.

b If I .... (know) the answer to your question, I .... (tell) you.

c I .... (gain) lots of experience if I .... (volunteer) for the project – but I didn't apply.

d If visibility .... (not/be) poor last night, the flight .... (leave) on time.

e .... (let) me know if you .... (like) me to cook dinner tonight.

f If Jack .... (not/work) so hard at university, he .... (not/get) such a good degree.

Listening Part 3 Multiple choice

1 What do you already know about 'artificial intelligence'? Do you think these developments in technology are important for our lives?

2 🎧 You will hear a radio interview with Paul Williams, an expert in artificial intelligence. For questions 1–6, choose the answer which fits best according to what you hear.

1 Paul explains that predictions made about AI in the past
   A turned out to be surprisingly accurate.
   B proved to be a long way off-target.
   C overestimated the demand for computers.
   D underestimated the 'brain power' of computers.

2 According to Paul, how do most experts feel about the future of AI?
   A convinced it could soon govern every aspect of our lives
   B uncertain what impact it might eventually have on our lives
   C worried that its development may get out of control
   D certain that its full effects will not be seen for some time yet

3 Paul feels that the comparison of AI and the arrival of the computer industry
   A shows that both industries are at a similar state of development.
   B illustrates that the computer industry was more popular in its time than AI.
   C misrepresents the true role of AI in our lives.
   D proves that the computer industry was a much more profitable concern.

4 What does Paul believe people's attitudes were to new technology in the 1900s?
   A They were very excited about its potential.
   B They had little idea what impact it would have.
   C They were suspicious of how it might change their lives.
   D They expected it to develop more quickly than it did.

5 Paul is slightly worried by the fact that machines which have intelligence could
   A one day kill off human beings.
   B rapidly assume human roles.
   C eventually replace humans in the workplace.
   D be running our lives in the near future.

6 What conclusion does Paul finally reach?
   A Science fiction is closer to reality than we think.
   B Intelligent machines will be able to feel emotions.
   C AI will develop more rapidly than we can ever imagine.
   D We should not be afraid that technology will take over our lives.

Use of English Part 1 Multiple-choice cloze

1 Read the article below, ignoring the gaps, about a survey into volunteering.
Why do people and businesses want to become involved?

2 For questions 1–12, read the article again and decide which answer (A, B, C or D) best fits each gap.

WHAT'S IN IT FOR ME?

Students and jobseekers keen to get onto the course or into the workplace of their
(0) ...B... , hope that voluntary work will help them (1) .... from the crowd.
This chance to (2) .... experience – personally and professionally – is
(3) .... on the wish-list of young people.

A survey carried out last year revealed that young and old (4) .... said
volunteering had improved their lives, particularly those (5) .... in conservation
or heritage work.

Businesses recognise its importance and get to (6) .... their profile in the
community, while staff get a break from their daily routine to develop 'soft skills',
(7) .... initiative and decision-making. One volunteering organisation is
(8) .... another survey to find out if volunteering does make a difference in the
workplace, or if it is something businesses do simply to improve their (9) ....

Not (10) .... are business-sponsored placements becoming more common, the
government is also investing money and aiming to (11) .... volunteers. The push
is clearly on to make volunteering as attractive as possible to everyone.
And the more people who participate, the more the act fulfils its (12) .... of
making the world a better place.

0	A alternative	B choice	C option	D election
1	A stand out	B lift out	C pick out	D point out
2	A win	B achieve	C collect	D gain
3	A extreme	B high	C sharp	D strong
4	A similar	B the same	C alike	D too
5	A committed	B associated	C connected	D involved
6	A raise	B increase	C arouse	D motivate
7	A such	B such as	C such like	D such and such
8	A governing	B guiding	C conducting	D directing
9	A representation	B look	C image	D figure
10	A only	B just	C merely	D simply
11	A claim	B recruit	C bring	D enter
12	A aim	B direction	C mark	D design

It's a crime

 9

Reading

Part 4 Multiple matching

1 Quickly read the text about book reviews and find out in which country each novel is set.

2 Read the text again and decide in which paragraph (A–F) the following are mentioned. The paragraphs may be chosen more than once.

a protagonist who fears he/she may be killed	1 ... 2 ...
the best novel the writer has written so far	3 ...
a desire to make international literature more accessible	4 ...
a novel that is impossible to stop reading	5 ...
an era which is accurately captured by the writer	6 ...
a crime against a family of considerable importance	7 ...
a storyline that deliberately misleads the reader	8 ...
a plot that includes a family	9 ... 10 ... 11 ...
a character who can move between social classes	12 ... 13 ...
a more optimistic story than the author usually writes	14 ...
a protagonist who wishes to have a say in politics	15 ...

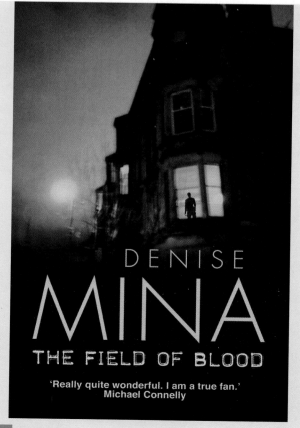

FAMILIES

A

In Denise Mina's *The Field of Blood*, it's 1981 and Paddy Meeham, eighteen, is determined that her lowly job as a copygirl on a Scottish newspaper will be her first step to becoming a reporter. It's an aspiration that
5 separates her from her working-class Catholic parents, who are suspicious of ambition and want everything to continue as it always has. When two small boys are arrested for the murder of a toddler, Paddy believes that the police don't have the whole story, and conducts
10 her own investigation. But this is not simply a murder mystery. Mina produces something special every time and this book – her finest yet – offers a memorable portrait of a touching heroine, along with the dynamics of the workplace and, especially, the family.

B

15 Barbara Vine uses crime as only one element in her
books. She is in unusually gentle mood in *The
Minotaur*, in which a Swedish woman describes an
unsettling experience that happened over 30 years
ago, when she was engaged to look after the grown-
20 up son of a bizarre English household. The once
grand, now shabby house, is ruled by a tyrannical old
woman, whose three unmarried daughters lead
separate, dismal lives, moving cautiously around
their autistic brother. The narrative is as compelling,
25 but not as dark, as we have come to expect from this
distinguished author.

C

The latest addition to Bitter Lemon Press is prize-
winning Cuban novelist Leonardo Padura. He does
nothing to hinder their mission to publish English
30 translations of the best foreign crime fiction. *Havana
Red*, the first book in his Havana quartet, introduces
Lieutenant Mario Conde – an eccentric personality
with unusual investigative methods. All his skills are
called upon when a murder victim turns out to be
35 the son of a prominent diplomat. Padura's powerful
writing creates an atmospheric picture of a turbulent
city, illuminated by Conde's mocking commentary.

AND OTHER
CRIMINALS

D

Jess Walter continues to impress with his new novel
Citizen Vince, which takes place in the run-up to the
40 1980 US Presidential election. His protagonist, Vince
Camden, is a life-long criminal who has avoided
another prison sentence by giving evidence against
other criminals. He is in witness protection,
contentedly managing a doughnut shop, while
45 keeping his hand in with a little credit card fraud,
when he discovers that his life is in danger. Vince
suddenly realises not only that he enjoys his new life
but that, for the first time, it is important to him to
vote in an election. His attempts to dodge his assassin
50 and pay off his debts so that he can cast his vote make
a splendidly entertaining, thoughtful book.

BLUE RONDO
John Lawton

'Lawton's trick – superbly executed – is to take
the threads of history and weave them into his
own tapestry.' *The Times*

E

John Lawton's post-Second World War series features
the London-based policeman Frederick Troy. Troy is
upper-class and his friends and colleagues include
55 both influential figures of society, and faithful
(though sometimes less than law-abiding) members
of the lower classes. Lawton's plots are tough and
Troy spends much of his time in hospital or getting to
know various female characters. In *Blue Rondo*, we
60 have reached the 1950s and Troy, now a Chief
Superintendent, is investigating a gangland war whilst
recovering from yet another injury and … other
subplots! Lawton's period atmosphere, illustrated
with credible characters, is impeccable and the
65 writing elegantly precise.

F

Harlan Coben has made his intentions clear: he
wants to give his protagonist – the good guy – a hard
time. And he makes a good job of doing so in *The
Innocent*. Everything is going well for Matt Hunter;
70 he has a great job, his wife is expecting their first
baby, and they have their ideal American home. But
then he finds his life and marriage inexplicably
threatened by an unknown man. The enjoyably
intricate plot takes several turns, involving a
75 videotape, FBI agents, and even a dead nun, before
we are taken on a final twist when the villains and
motive are revealed. A book you can't help reading in
one go.

Vocabulary

Phrasal verbs: multiple particles

1 Read the different definitions for phrasal verbs with *fall*. Then use your dictionary to find the correct particle for each definition a–g.

	a	be tricked into believing something that is not true
	b	have something to use when you are in difficulty
	c	try very hard or want very much to do something
fall	d	to not be completed or not happen
	e	fail to keep up with something
	f	decrease in quality or quantity
	g	have an argument with someone so that you are no longer friendly with them

2 Complete dialogues 1–7 using the phrasal verbs from 1.

1   A: I'm afraid I've .... with my work this week.
     B: Oh, you'll easily catch up over the weekend.

2   A: Did you manage to find anyone interested in joining the student committee?
     B: Not really – people weren't exactly .... We have to make it sound more appealing.

3   A: What on earth will I do if the new business is not a success?
     B: You can always .... your teaching qualifications – don't worry!

4   A: Did you get that job you wanted with the travel agency?
     B: I didn't. At the last minute the whole thing .... because they filled the vacancy with an internal candidate.

5   A: Do you get on well with the neighbours?
     B: No. We .... over a year ago and we haven't spoken since.

6   A: I can't believe that you .... that story about Jack being a pilot.
     B: Neither can I – but it seemed plausible at the time.

7   A: Why isn't the football team getting any funding now?
     B: Well, hardly anyone is going to the matches. Attendance has really .... over the last few months.

Grammar

Passives

1 Read the text about an arts academy. Then rewrite each sentence beginning with the words in bold and using the passive form.

BOWLANDS ACADEMY OF ARTS

Someone established **Bowlands Academy of Arts** five years ago. The Department of Education has now officially recognised **the establishment**. The academy offers students **a programme of short, intensive courses**, as well as three-year degree courses. Students can take **a range of examinations** throughout the year. Staff instruct **students** in small groups and they assign every student a personal tutor. Anyone requiring **accommodation in a hall of residence** must book it in advance. Students need to enclose **a deposit** with the enrolment form. The Academy will request **the balance** before the course starts. Students need to inform **the Academy** immediately if they intend to withdraw from their course.

Example
Bowlands Academy of Arts was established five years ago.

2 Complete dialogues 1–7 using the prompts in brackets and a verb from below in the correct form.

> steal   service   investigate   confiscate
> pierce   dry-clean   test

1   A: I can't read the small print in this document.
    B: Maybe you should go to the optician's and .... (get/eyes) ....

2   A: What's Jill done to herself? She looks different.
    B: It's the earrings. She .... (have/ears) .... last week.

3   A: Look at this stain on my sleeve!
    B: You'll have to .... (get/jacket) ....

4   A: I'd forgotten I had this pair of scissors in my hand-luggage.
    B: They're bound to .... (get) .... by airport security staff.

5   A: The engine won't start.
    B: I don't believe it. We only .... (have/car) .... last week.

6   A: The central locking's broken so I've had to leave the car unlocked.
    B: Let's hope it .... (not/get) ....

7   A: Have you heard anything more about that enormous tax bill you were sent?
    B: Actually, I .... (have/matter) .... by my accountant at this very moment.

3 Rewrite statements a–e using the passive form of the word in italics and beginning with the prompts given.

a   There's a *rumour* that the government is going to resign.
    It ....

b   Financial experts *predict* interest rates are about to rise.
    Interest rates ....

c   Everyone *assumed* the missing gangland leader had been murdered.
    The missing ....

d   They *think* the plane crash was due to human error.
    It ....

e   People *believe* terrorists are hiding out in the north of the country.
    Terrorists ....

Listening Part 1 Short extracts

1 Discuss these questions which relate to the extracts in exercise 2.

    a   What types of discipline are typically used in schools in your country?

    b   Is antisocial behaviour a problem in schools or in public places where you live? How do you think this should be dealt with?

2 🎧 Read questions 1–6 below before you listen to the three different extracts. Then listen and choose the answer (A, B or C) which fits best according to what you hear.

You hear part of an interview with a teacher talking about 'the cooler room'.

1 'The cooler room' has attracted a lot of publicity because it
    A is seen as a controversial punishment.
    B has a link with a famous film.
    C shows an old-fashioned approach to discipline.

2 The punishment has been effective because pupils
    A dislike being constantly watched.
    B do not like being on their own.
    C hate the restrictions imposed on them.

You hear two people on a current affairs programme talking about ASBOs (Antisocial Behaviour Orders).

3 What do ASBOs do?
    A give a short prison sentence
    B offer help to offenders
    C restrict people's movements

4 The problem with ASBOs is that they
    A are not always obeyed.
    B can be given to the wrong people.
    C do not last long enough.

You hear part of an interview with a woman from the Witness Support Programme.

5 Why can giving evidence be distressing?
    A It's frightening to face criminals.
    B It's something you can't prepare for.
    C It can bring back bad memories.

6 The majority of people who work on the Programme
    A work unusual hours.
    B do not receive payment.
    C have special training.

Use of English Part 2 Open cloze

1 Read the description below of the film *Inside Man* and find out what type of film it is.

2 For questions 1–15, read the text again and think of the word which best fits each gap.

INSIDE **MAN**

A team of acclaimed actors (0) ...*come*.... together to explore the lure of power and the ugliness of greed (1) .... this fast-paced crime drama – *Inside Man*.

The key players (2) .... Denzil Washington as a newly promoted detective (3) .... must rise above a corruption scandal, Clive Owen as a brilliant criminal making us question what we think we know (4) .... bank robberies, and Jodie Foster as a mysterious Manhattan businesswoman looking after her (5) ....:.. interests.

They play the roles (6) .... tough New Yorkers who have to outwit (7) .... another to protect their competing interests in this skilfully penned thriller (8) .... director Spike Lee. (9) .... of the characters represent tiny pieces of a complex interlocking puzzle, but is every piece (10) .... it seems?

It's difficult (11) .... define this film precisely. There's a celebration of heist films and police corruption movies from (12) .... 1970s, but it's also slick and modern and full of fancy tricks of the camera and plot twists (13) .... continually tease the audience every step of the way. *Inside Man* reveals (14) .... as anything but the typical thriller and can only (15) .... described as unmissable.

Part 5 Key word transformations

3 Rewrite the second sentence in a–c keeping the meaning the same.
Use three to six words including the word given.

a You probably won't find a better deal for a holiday.
  CHANCES
  The .... find a better deal for a holiday.

b Paul is trying desperately to get a promotion.
  OVER
  Paul is .... to get a promotion.

c The issue will be investigated next week without fail.
  LOOKED
  The issue is .... next week without fail.

Review Units 7–9

1 Match 1–6 with a–e to make compound adjectives.

1	narrow-	a	handed
2	self-	b	time
3	down	c	hearted
4	first-	d	minded
5	open-	e	made
6	light-		

2 Complete the text about astronomy by putting the words in brackets into a suitable participle form.

1 (peer) .... for years across 1,500 light years of space, scientists now believe they may have found an explanation for creation. 2 (use) .... a sophisticated telescope, scientists have studied hundreds of stars, 3 (identify) .... 27 that behave as the sun did 4.6 billion years ago. The nine planets around the sun were the only ones 4 (know) .... in the whole universe, but 5 (make) .... use of recent observations, astronomers then began to detect other planets. 6 (conclude) .... their research, scientists believe they may have discovered the beginnings of earth-like planets.

3 Complete these sentences using the correct form of *fall* with a suitable particle.

a What's it like to be head-over-heels in love? I've never .... anybody.

b Never .... with your studies. If you do, you'll never catch up.

c When the sale started, crowds of customers were .... to grab a bargain.

d The skiing trip .... in the end, as it proved too complicated to arrange.

e Things haven't been so pleasant here since we .... with the neighbours in the flat above.

f Surely you didn't .... that ridiculous story? It was obvious he was lying!

4 Complete sentences a–f with words formed by adding suffixes to 1–6.

1 neighbour
2 care
3 act
4 employ
5 friend
6 child

a Sally won .... of the month at her office!

b I think socialising and forming new .... are the most enjoyable parts of my life.

c I spent my .... in Scotland; it was an amazing place to grow up.

d Nicole Kidman is my favourite .... I adore all her films.

e This .... is very exclusive; it's an extremely affluent area.

f He is unbelievably .... with his work and continuously makes mistakes.

5 For questions a–c, think of one word only which can be used appropriately in all three sentences.

a Did you .... out with Andrew? Why aren't you two speaking?
If you .... behind with your schedule, you will be in trouble.
A good education is something to .... back on when you need it.

b It all came to a .... when Julie discovered the box of old letters.
The newly appointed .... of the department addressed the school warmly.
Shaking his .... in total disbelief, the coach left the pitch.

c The .... of your course fees must be paid by December.
You need excellent .... as well as grace to be a dancer.
Health experts agree that a .... between work and leisure should be encouraged.

6 Write the correct phrasal verb with *off* or *in* for definitions a–g.

a understand or remember sth   t....... ....
b try to impress people   s....... ....
c ask for sb's services   c....... ....
d suddenly become successful   t....... ....
e introduce a new law   b....... ....
f interrupt sb when speaking   c....... ....
g succeed in doing sth difficult b....... ....

7 Add the correct negative prefix to adjectives 1–8, then match them with synonyms a–h.

1 ....tolerable   a inaccessible
2 ....reversible   b inhospitable
3 ....stable   c indistinguishable
4 ....sensitive   d insecure
5 ....sociable   e incalculable
6 ....penetrable   f unbearable
7 ....perceptible   g uncaring
8 ....measurable   h unchangeable

8 Underline the correct conditional form in sentences a–g.

a If I *would have/had* enough free time, I would do voluntary work.
b If she *asks/had asked* me, I'll consider helping out at the festival.
c If they *had left/leave* home earlier, they would not have missed the train.
d If students *read/would read* English newspapers, it helps improve their vocabulary.
e If you *see/had seen* Ben this morning, remind him to pick up those tickets.
f If I *went/had visited* Australia, I might have emigrated permanently.
g If the restaurant *was/wasn't* so expensive, we could go there for our anniversary.

9 Complete gaps a–g in the table with the correct form of the words given.

noun	adjective
a	content
b anxiety	....
c clarity	....
d	secret
e diplomacy	....
f	authentic
g democracy	....

10 Correct the mistakes in the passive form in a–g.

a The package was arrived safely and on schedule this morning.
b Tonight's recital is been given by a well-known pianist.
c Exhibit 451 is being thought to have been painted by Picasso.
d This violin is to be considered the best example of a period instrument of this kind.
e I can't stand having made to do what I consider to be a waste of time.
f A collection of priceless gold coins has being discovered in a castle on the south coast.
g According to the police, this building could have abandoned for some time.

11 Rewrite the second sentence in a–c keeping the meaning the same. Use three to six words including the word given.

a Remote parts of the country always become isolated in severe weather.
   CUT
   Remote parts of the country ....
   .... in severe weather.
b Apparently the entire warehouse was destroyed in a fire last month.
   UP
   Apparently the entire warehouse ....
   .... last month.
c You should go for an eye test if you're struggling to read the newspaper.
   TESTED
   You should ....
   if you're struggling to read the newspaper.

Buying and selling

Reading Part 2 Gapped text

1 Quickly read the article about the textile industry in China. What facts or figures do you find surprising?

2 Read the article again. Six paragraphs have been removed from the extract. Choose from the paragraphs A–G the one which fits each gap (1–6). There is one extra paragraph.

dressing for **success**

The next time you get dressed, cast your mind eastwards towards Qiaotou. For no matter whether you are wearing bell-bottomed jeans, a pencil skirt or tailored trousers, the chances are that the button or zip comes from this dusty, dirty town. Located in the middle of nowhere, this is the sort of place you might drive through without noticing. It is too small to be marked on most western maps of China, too insignificant to merit a mention in newspapers, and barely known outside the local area. But in just twenty-five years, this humble community has destroyed most of its international rivals to become the undisputed global capital of buttons and zips.

1 ....

The commercial revolution here is on a scale and at a pace that exceeds anything experienced before. The first small workshop was established in 1980 by three brothers who picked their first buttons off the street. Now the town's 700 family-run factories churn out 15 billion buttons and 200 million metres of zips a year. The low-investment, labour-intensive industry was ideal for this remote community. And it could not have timed its rise better. Qiaotou began popping buttons just as China started dressing up. Out went the Mao suits, and in came chic western clothes. So this is the place to head for if you're looking for a button of exactly the right shape, size and material, to adorn those new fashions hanging in your wardrobe.

2 ....

Such mind-boggling export statistics, until recently, were used as evidence of the Chinese miracle. Now, however, the global domination of manufacturing towns such as this is increasingly being discussed in very different terms: as a sign of a threat to other manufacturing countries. After the Cultural Revolution, the world cheered on the market-oriented reforms. Growth of more than 9% a year for more than two decades has lifted hundreds of millions out of poverty. Consumers across the globe have benefited from the cheap goods made by factory workers in Qiaotou and elsewhere.

3 ....

But Chinese businessmen are unfazed by this action. 'Even if we lose a few customers in the short term, they will have to come back,' says the president of the Great Wall Zipper group. 'There is almost nowhere else in the world that makes zips.'

4 ....

Take, for instance, Yiwu. If China is the workshop of the world, Yiwu is its showroom. Selling
50 everything from engine parts to hair clips and costume jewellery, this town's market has grown from a few dozen street stalls ten years ago to become the world's biggest commodity trading centre.

5 ....

55 And it is hard to imagine that this worldwide monopoly will end any time soon; Lanswe, the biggest sock manufacturer in the world, spins out two million socks a day. Within two years the company plans to triple its workforce to 15,000
60 and increase output to five million socks a day. Textile quotas or no textile quotas, half of them are destined for export.

6 ....

The view from China is that foreign countries say they want China to develop, but when it does,
65 they become nervous. China is changing. The countryside is changing and change is a cause for hope. But China needs to be given time to make sure its miracle does not sour.

A

And buyers do indeed come here from all over the
70 world. Attracted by prices of less than a penny a zip and the decent quality, international retail outlets and fashion houses are increasingly purchasing from Qiaotou. The local chamber of commerce estimates that three out of every five buttons in the world are
75 made in the town, which boasts 1,300 button shops selling 1,400 varieties of buttons. It ships more than two million zips a day, making it the biggest winner of China's 80% share of the international zip market.

B

Talk of unfair currency manipulation and the need
80 for trade quotas is nothing new. The domination of the world markets for cars and electronics in the 1980s led to a fierce trade dispute and pressure for appreciation of the yen. When this eventually did happen, the flood of money into the country inflated
85 an enormous speculative bubble in the early 90s.

C

And what was once a modest farming village is now a manufacturing powerhouse – a microcosm of what has happened to the entire Chinese economy in the last few decades. It is a familiar story: paddy fields
90 have been cleared for factories and peasants have become industrialists. The river, which used to be a clean source for irrigation, is now a heavily polluted outlet for brightly coloured plastic waste.

D

The same confidence prevails throughout the south
95 coastal provinces. With endless streets of giant factories and company dormitories, the most developed areas are modern-day equivalents of Western cities at the peak of the Industrial Revolution. The many small towns, some not even
100 on maps, have become world-beaters by focusing on labour-intensive niches.

E

The company's president says he can understand why countries want to restrict this growth and impose certain limits, even though it might hurt his
105 business. 'Even if the yuan gets stronger, rich countries will still import socks because they cannot make them cheaply enough themselves.' He believes that, in the long run, change must come through market forces rather than export quotas and
110 currency manipulation. 'If rich nations really want to compete with China, they need to make us richer. That's the best way to make prices rise here.'

F

After a decade of towns like this one growing almost unnoticed, the world has suddenly realised just how
115 powerful they have become. Thanks to globalisation, the clothes of the world are being zipped and buttoned up by deft-fingered migrant workers, our teeth are being brushed with bristles from Huang Zi, and our toes are being kept warm by the products of
120 Yiwu.

G

But recently, the rejoicing has been replaced by warnings. A flood of Chinese goods has swept into European and American markets, threatening jobs and alarming governments. One administration
125 responded by setting a limit on shipments of jackets, trousers and shirts. Others have taken a less aggressive line, by setting quotas to protect their clothing industries from the competition in China.

Vocabulary

Money

1 The three words given in each of 1–4 have a
similar meaning. Complete sentences a and b with
the most suitable word from the three given.

1 fees/invoices/fares
   a Taxi .... usually increase dramatically
     after midnight.
   b Entrance .... to the gallery are reduced
     for students.

2 bill/receipt/cheque
   a You will need to obtain a .... to claim
     your expenses.
   b I didn't expect to receive such a large
     .... !

3 pay/salary/wage
   a The introduction of the minimum ....
     was welcomed by all employees.
   b His annual .... fell just below the
     national average.

4 cash/change/tip
   a We need to resolve the business's ....
     flow problems within the next month.
   b Do you have any loose .... to pay for
     the coffees?

2 Complete sentences a–d with words from 1 in the
correct form.

   a .... for manual work are still way behind
     those of skilled workers.
   b Tuition .... are one of many issues facing
     students today.
   c Have you got some .... to leave a tip for
     the waiter?
   d Make sure that you get a .... when you
     pay for the goods.

Word formation (3)

3 Write the verb forms of a–i, ending in -ate, -en, or
-ify. Use your dictionary to help you.

   a false   ....
   b strength   ....
   c activity   ....
   d broad   ....
   e typical   ....
   f alternative   ....
   g demonstration ....
   h sad   ....
   i peace   ....

4 Use the verbs from 3 in the correct form to
complete these sentences.

   a Opposition to our plans .... and increased
     our determination to put them into action.
   b To be fluent in another language, you should
     .... the vocabulary you learn by using it
     as often as possible.
   c It later became apparent that the documentation
     had been .... and we had all been misled.
   d The mood of the waiting crowd ....
     between boredom and anger.
   e Can you find a way to .... the region and
     resolve the conflict?
   f We were all .... to hear about the loss of
     your grandfather, and send our sympathy.
   g After working in the same city for ten years, I
     decided to .... my horizons and travel the
     world.

Grammar Mixed conditionals

1 Make conditional sentences from the boxes below. There may be more than one possibility.

a Permission for the event will not be given	it's an emergency.
b What you may have done in the past is not important	unless
c I never use my mobile phone	provided
d Would you agree to the scheme	as long as
e Jim would never have changed his job	supposing

a Permission for the event will not be given
b What you may have done in the past is not important
c I never use my mobile phone
d Would you agree to the scheme
e Jim would never have changed his job

unless
provided
as long as
supposing

it's an emergency.
you are honest with me now.
I wanted you to be involved in it?
he'd been forced to.
all safety regulations are complied with.

2 Choose the correct option, a or b, to complete sentences 1–7.

1 I wish I .... afford to upgrade my computer system.
   a would be able to   b could

2 My brother wishes he .... the firm he is currently working for.
   a didn't join   b hadn't joined

3 Don't you wish you .... speak more languages fluently?
   a could   b would

4 If only my boss .... me to work all day long.
   a haven't expected   b didn't expect

5 Do you ever wish you .... to go somewhere else on holiday?
   a had chosen   b chose

6 If only people .... keep interrupting me in mid-sentence!
   a won't   b wouldn't

7 I wish I .... to your advice.
   a wouldn't listen   b hadn't listened

Grammar Extra Determiners

3 Circle the correct determiner to complete sentences a–j.

a *The whole/All the* idea of raising money to keep run-down museums open seems pointless.
b There is *not many/hardly any* good news in the media these days.
c The question of whether we can actually help developing countries by giving aid is a difficult *one/other*.
d *None/Neither* of the advice that Charlotte offered was useful to me.
e *Every/Each* of the paintings on loan for the exhibition has been insured against damage.
f Unfortunately, due to my family commitments, I have *a little/little* time to myself these days.
g *Loads/Several* of people came to the opening of the Italian restaurant.
h Some traffic restrictions do prevent accidents, whereas *others/another* merely cause traffic jams.
i Fortunately, *a few/few* people managed to make it to work yesterday, despite the atrocious weather conditions.
j The *most/whole* we can do is hope they don't notice our mistakes.

Listening Part 3 Multiple choice

1 What problems or consequences do you think 'music piracy' (illegally obtaining music) may cause?

2 🎧 You will hear an interview with a journalist, Sam Broadbent, who is talking about music piracy. For questions 1–6, choose the correct answers.

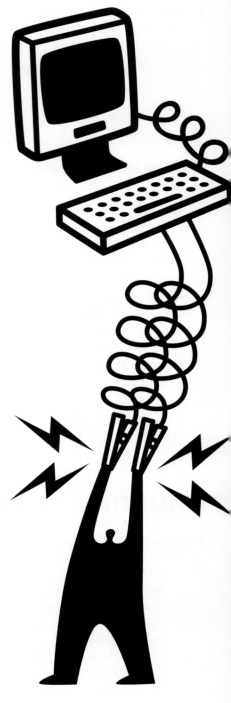

1 According to Sam, the issue of music piracy is complicated because
   A too many private individuals are being taken to court.
   B it's unclear who should actually be prosecuted.
   C it's difficult to prevent people buying the necessary software.
   D the entertainment industry is making downloading too desirable.

2 What happened in one legal case in 1984?
   A The use of video recorders was banned in certain places.
   B The entertainment industry successfully sued a video manufacturer.
   C It was decided that the main purpose of video recording was not illegal.
   D A video manufacturer was found guilty of making illegal copies of films.

3 Sam says the current legal case
   A concentrates on the many people losing their income.
   B doesn't question how the products are used.
   C is targeting the firms that enable people to download illegally.
   D suggests the banning of illegal products.

4 What is Sam's greatest fear?
   A People will stop worrying about whether downloading is right or wrong.
   B The development of downloading technology will be slowed.
   C People in the entertainment industry will no longer be active.
   D Manufacturers of new technology will constantly be involved in lawsuits.

5 According to Sam, many members of the public he has talked to feel that
   A copyright laws should be further tightened.
   B the products they buy could be less expensive.
   C the entertainment industry is losing out financially.
   D distribution costs should be passed on to the manufacturers.

6 In Sam's opinion, films should be released
   A much more quickly on DVD.
   B in Europe before being released in the USA.
   C on the Internet and at the cinema at the same time.
   D in cinemas all over the world simultaneously.

Use of English

Part 3 Word formation

1 Read the article below about 'Freecycle' and find out what it is and how it started.

2 For questions 1–10, read the text again and use the words given in capitals to form a word.

Giving it away

Resisting the (0) ....**temptation**.......... to buy is hard, be it a new outfit, gadget or a little treat. Now guilty shoppers keen to get rid of (1) .... purchases have a new option – simply give it away online. As the name suggests, everything advertised on Freecycle must be free and whether it's CDs, old jeans or even a few hours' help in the garden, it'll be (2) .... to someone! Anyone interested just replies by email and the deal goes ahead. Freecycle is just one website which is playing an (3) .... role in reducing the amount of rubbish sent to landfill sites, through the (4) .... of a more efficient form of recycling – (5) .... giving things to people who want them.

The site is the (6) .... of Deron Beal, an (7) .... from Arizona, who started it as a list on the Internet. Today it resembles a cross between an Internet auction house and a (8) .... chain of charity shops. Beal says his chief aim is to cut waste and help the environment. 'I live in a beautiful desert area,' Beal recently explained to (9) .... , 'and in the middle of it you've got this hideous landfill, overflowing with good, reusable stuff.' The Freecycle network now has over a million members throughout the world. So, if you want a (10) .... good sofa, and the owner lives nearby, it can be picked up rather than posted!

0	TEMPT	6	CREATE
1	WANT	7	ENVIRONMENT
2	VALUE	8	GLOBE
3	ACT	9	REPORT
4	PROMOTE	10	PERFECT
5	SIMPLE		

Part 4 Gapped sentences

3 Think of one word only which can be used appropriately in all three sentences. The word appears in the text opposite.

She screamed for .... and luckily someone heard her.

Thanks for all your .... through such a difficult time.

Practical .... is offered through our accommodation service to new students.

4 Which word below can be used in each of a–c?

■ brawl   fight   attack

a There was a violent .... in the town centre last night.
b Our local team put up a great .... , but it wasn't enough to win the match.
c The .... against crime continues to dominate the news.

5 Look up the two words not used in 4 in your dictionary. Which one has more uses and meanings?

Entertainment or art?

Reading

Part 1 Themed texts

1 Read the three extracts opposite quickly and decide if the writers' attitudes towards the subjects are positive, neutral, or negative.

2 For questions 1–6, read the extracts again and choose the answer (A, B, C or D) which you think fits best according to the text.

Public art or public eyesore?

You could be forgiven for wondering exactly what a giant pink rabbit on an Italian mountainside and an enormous table and chair in a London park have to do with art. You would not be alone. A certain
05 amount of debate surrounds the relatively recent increase in what is known as 'installation art'. But, then again – when has art ever been free from controversy?

The term 'Installation art' is used today to refer to works of art constructed outdoors that are usually temporary and often
10 very large. Hence we had Neri's 'The Writer' on Parliament Hill in London in 2006, an enormous table and chair with an inspirational view for an unseen 'writer'. This was a temporary installation, lasting only a few months, unlike the art group Gelatin's 'pink rabbit' which is intended to remain on a
15 mountainside until 2025, encouraging art lovers to clamber all over it and sleep on its stomach. Another artist, Rachel Whiteread, made headlines in 1993 when she won the Turner Prize for 'House', a cast of the interior of a Victorian house. This work was destroyed after a very short time but Antony Gormley's 'Another Place' (a
20 collection of 100 bronze replicas of himself) has been moved from one site to another around the world and he would like it to find a permanent home in Merseyside.

These are just a few examples of an art form that is becoming popular worldwide – the common theme being the artist's desire
25 for their work to interact with the immediate environment in some way. For many people it is a hugely exciting concept. For others the installations are simply huge eyesores. Whatever we think, they are definitely too large to be ignored.

1 'Installation art' is controversial because
A it is often sited in dangerous places.
B some people don't consider the works to be real art.
C people think the structures are too large.
D they are often not permanent structures.

2 What do installation artists aim to do?
A draw attention to social issues through their work
B exhibit their work in unappealing locations
C allow people to enjoy art without paying
D make the locations and settings part of their work

BA IN ACTING

COURSE OUTLINE

30 The three year BA in Acting lasts for nine terms, which vary in length from eleven to twelve weeks. It is
35 intended for students who wish to earn a living working in theatre, film, television and radio. It is an
40 arduous course, with classes running from 10 am to 6.30 pm and individual classes later in the evening. During public performances the working day can be from 10 am
45 to 11 pm. Students are continuously assessed and regular feedback sessions with individual tutors are an integral part of the course.

The aim of this intensive training is to develop individual skills at the highest level and equip students
50 with the necessary expertise to cope with the course and the demanding world of professional acting.

AUDITIONS

There is an intake of up to 32 students in September each year, with auditions from October to April.
55 Late applications are not accepted under any circumstances. Candidates are given an option of auditioning in London or New York. London auditions are held continuously thoughout this period. Candidates auditioning in Manchester
60 should be prepared to attend subsequent recalls and workshops in London if required. It is RADA's policy to audition all candidates who apply before the closing date for the BA in Acting. A list of audition guidance notes will be sent to all applicants.

The Dark Tower VII

65 This magnificent novel is the final volume in Stephen King's epic masterpiece and the most anticipated book in his
70 legendary career. It is the book millions of his readers have been waiting for with excitement and awe in their own quest to reach the
75 Dark Tower. Powerful and darkly suspenseful, this unforgettable finale will also leave readers wanting to read the series again.

80 The last masterful chapter of Roland Deschain's relentless quest is a roller-coaster of exhilarating triumph and aching loss. Roland's band of pilgrims remains united, though scattered. Susannah-Mia has been carried off to a chamber in New York. Jake,
85 Father Callahan and even Oy follow, not aware of how deadly are the foes that they face. Roland and Eddie are in Maine, looking for the site on Turtleback Lane which will lead them to Susannah.

His every move shadowed by a terrible and sinister
90 creation, Roland closes in on the Tower. And finally he realises he may have to leave his companions in the last dark strait.

Thus the book opens, like a door, to the uttermost reaches of Stephen King's imagination. You've come
95 this far. Come a little farther. Come all the way. The sound you hear may be the slamming of the door behind you. Welcome to *The Dark Tower*.

---

3 Students who take the BA in acting must
  A be prepared to put in very long hours.
  B accept work in alternative entertainment industries.
  C take examinations on a regular basis.
  D have previous experience of acting professionally.

4 What information is given to prospective applicants?
  A An audition venue will be allocated in one of three places.
  B The course can be joined at any point after October.
  C Applications after the closing date will not be considered.
  D Guidance notes are provided at the audition venue.

5 Why have Stephen King's fans been waiting eagerly for this book?
  A He has been writing it for a long time.
  B The story line of the novel is reported as the most ingenious yet.
  C A film will be released shortly after the book is published.
  D It is the culmination of previous stories.

6 In this description of *The Dark Tower*, we learn that
  A Roland may be taking the final step on his own.
  B the characters are finally united.
  C there is a tragic and unexpected death.
  D readers are expected to read the whole series first.

Vocabulary

Three-part phrasal verbs

1 Choose the correct verb in sentences a–h to make three-part phrasal verbs.

a We should *look/take/go* up to the older generation – they have so much wisdom.

b I'm afraid the job didn't *pull/live/move* up to my expectations so I decided to hand in my notice.

c Dad will just have to *look/face/sit* up to the fact that he's not as young as he used to be.

d The only way to deal with bullies is either to run away or *stand/push/call* up to them.

e No one *saw/felt/went* up to going to the concert so we stayed at home instead.

f Thanks for the lovely lunch. It's great to see you, but I'm afraid I've got to *get/take/move* back to work. Bye!

g There was so much to do in the week *going/leading/walking* up to the holiday, that we were exhausted when we finally got on the plane.

h Why don't you *start/wake/jump* up to the fact that you will never pass your exams, if you go out all the time?

2 Match phrasal verbs from 1 with meanings 1–8.

1 respect
2 have the energy to do something
3 return
4 confront someone
5 approach or prepare for something
6 accept and deal with something
7 be as good as expected
8 become aware of a situation

3 Make two three-part phrasal verbs from each of 1–3 below.

1	put	down up	with to
2	get come	down away	with
3	drop	in out	of on

4 Use your dictionary to answer the following questions about the phrasal verbs in 3.

a In which phrasal verb is the object placed before the particles?

b What other three-part phrasal verbs can you find for these verbs?

5 Use the phrasal verbs from 3 to replace the words in italics in a–f.

a We don't *tolerate* that kind of behaviour in this school.

b Not many people went to the exhibition. I *think* this *is because of* the location – it's really hard to find that gallery.

c In winter many elderly people *become ill with* the flu.

d How did Bob manage to *go unpunished for* forgetting his wedding anniversary?

e Almost half of the students *chose to stop going to* the debating society meetings.

f I'm just going to *quickly visit* Jill for a coffee – do you want to come along?

Grammar

Comparatives and superlatives

1 Correct the mistakes with comparatives and superlatives in sentences a–f.

a Have you read his latest novel? It's so boring and just as all the others.

b Sarah hated travelling by coach. In her opinion, it was by far the worse choice. The train was simply the best option.

c She's a lot as her sister. They're both extremely creative and have fiery tempers.

d The more time I spend travelling, the little I want to settle down in one place.

e Why don't we go to the modern art gallery on Thornton Street? It's far interesting than the other one.

f I've never had such a boring holiday. It was not near as good as I thought it would be.

2 Complete sentences a–h using the words below.

> just   no more   nothing   nowhere   great
> bit   nearly   slightly

a Booking online is only .... cheaper than booking by phone.

b According to the airlines, air travel is .... as safe as any other form of transport.

c Season tickets aren't .... as expensive as those bought on a daily basis.

d Buying decent quality sportswear is .... expensive than buying clothes with a designer label.

e Unfortunately, the band's latest album is .... near as good as their previous one.

f Learning to play the piano is .... like as difficult as learning to play the violin.

g If you worked a .... harder, you might actually achieve your objectives.

h Travelling alone is a .... deal more exciting than travelling in a group.

3 Choose four of the expressions in 2 and use them in sentences to compare
- watching DVDs or going to the cinema.
- listening to CDs and going to a concert.
- modern art and Renaissance art.

Grammar Extra

so and such

4 Complete sentences a–g using *so* or *such*.

a Fresh vegetables, ... as cauliflowers and aubergines, are available at the market.

b The measures have been introduced .... that safety standards can be improved.

c We consider ourselves fortunate to have .... friendly neighbours.

d Housing is expensive in the capital and .... is the cost of parking.

e 'Is Mike here yet?' 'Yes, I think ....'

f It was .... a complicated form that no one could understand how to fill it in.

g Fifty or .... people attended the lecture.

5 Match the examples of *so* and *such* in 4 with uses 1–6 below.

1 to give an example
2 to indicate that something is not exact
3 to say that something else is true
4 to emphasise
5 to offer an explanation
6 to avoid repeating a phrase

Listening

Part 2 Sentence completion

1 Which of the following do you think is necessary to show that you appreciate modern art?

- having a thorough knowledge of art
- obtaining a qualification in art
- creating your own works of art
- behaving in a certain manner at galleries
- owning works by famous artists

2 🎧 You will hear an expert giving some advice on art appreciation. For questions 1–8, complete the sentences.

how to appreciate modern art

Remember that modern art began around the year .... 1.

The aim of modern art was to rebel against .... 2.

It is essential to .... 3 at a gallery.

You need to wear .... 4 during your visit.

Never stand where the .... 5 interfere with your appreciation of a painting.

Remember that .... 6 is taken extremely seriously in galleries.

You can actually get a better view by .... 7 and using binoculars.

Make sure you only stop to look at .... 8 works of art.

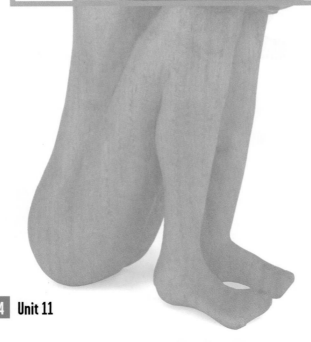

Use of English

Part 2 Open cloze

1 Quickly read the text below, about a new games machine.
Do you think this will still be popular in five years?

2 For questions 1–15, read the text again and think of the word which best fits each gap.

Wii tries to put the fun back

The games industry **0** ....**may**..... have lost sight of what video games are all
1 .... ; this is the charge levied by some critics who want more than amazing
graphics. After all, video games are not **2** .... about whizz-bang visuals, they
are also about **3** .... fun with your friends.

Nintendo have taken a step back **4** .... what their rivals are doing, and are
putting the focus on the games themselves and, **5** .... importantly, how we
play them. The result is the Wii.

The best thing about the new machine is its motion-sensing controller, a simple
device with hardly **6** .... buttons on it; it looks a lot **7** .... a TV remote control. It also comes with an
attachment for additional control in certain games. The Wii's games have been designed to **8** .... advantage of this
motion-sensing device. When this is coupled **9** .... the seamless gameplay and controller, it all adds **10** .... to a
thrilling gaming experience.

So **11** .... do you actually play? For tennis, you hit, smash or lob the ball **12** .... in a real game; in bowling
you roll the controller as you **13** .... roll a real ball. In other words, it's completely realistic – and lots of fun. The only
problem **14** .... far has been the number of accidents caused by players accidentally hitting one **15** .... with
the controller in the enthusiasm of playing!

Part 5 Key word transformations

3 Rewrite the second sentence in a–d keeping the meaning the same. Use three to six words including the
word given.

a I want to know if you have finalised those delivery dates yet?
ROUND
Have you .... those delivery dates yet?

b Unfortunately, if there is a rise in interest rates, we shall have to increase our prices.
EVENT
Unfortunately, ... a rise in interest rates, we shall have to increase our prices.

c Somehow no one found out he had stolen the technical design from another company.
AWAY
Somehow he .... the technical design from another company.

d After drama school my best friend became a big name on the stage.
ON
After drama school my best friend .... a big name on the stage.

A changing world

Reading Part 4 Multiple matching

1 Read the article about how to be environmentally friendly. Which summary of the writer's comments (a–c) is the most accurate?

a There are numerous ways to help the planet.
b It is pointless to try to follow schemes and ideas.
c We should be aware of unexpected consequences of our actions.

2 For questions 1–12, read the article again and choose in which paragraph (A–E) the following are mentioned. The paragraphs may be chosen more than once.

a controversial pastime that raises considerable money	1 …	
an action which creates a different weather pattern	2 …	
an undesirable result of unnecessary global transportation	3 …	4 …
inadequate research into harmful substances	5 …	
a continual change in what is required or needed	6 …	
people at the greatest risk from factors beyond their control	7 …	
a far-reaching change in official attitude	8 …	
a benefit for those the scheme was not originally intended for	9 …	10 …
the bringing of a source of energy to remote areas	11 …	
a failure to adapt in order to meet increasing demands	12 …	

But will it save the planet?

A Fair trade

Farmers in developing countries are some of the most vulnerable people on earth, prey to world commodity markets, middle men and the weather. So-called 'fair-trade' arrangements guarantee co-operative groups a
5 price above the world market and a bonus on top. The growing fair-trade market has distributed hundreds of millions of pounds to more than 50 million people worldwide. But critics say that fair trade will never lift a country out of poverty; indeed, it may keep it there,
10 because the money generated from sales goes almost in its entirety to rich countries which promote the products. As a simple guide, only about 5% of the sale price of a fair-trade chocolate bar may actually go to the poor country.

B Organic food

15 For food to be organic it must be free of added chemicals, both in the growing of the food and in the killing of the pests that might damage the crop. In a world where many manufactured chemicals have never been properly tested for safety, this is a very big selling
20 point. Parents are thus prepared to pay a premium for organic food, especially when chemicals suspected of causing a variety of problems have been found, albeit in tiny quantities, in most children's blood. The problem is that many farmers have not switched to
25 organic in sufficient numbers to satisfy this growing market. As a result, supermarkets are often forced to fly vegetables they can label 'organic' halfway round the world, at a great cost to the planet in extra greenhouse gases. Environmentalists are now urging shoppers to
30 buy locally produced vegetables, even if they are not organic and have been sprayed with pesticides.

C Recycling

A great shift has taken place in the way we think about rubbish. Where once we were happy to bury it in landfills or dump it at sea, we are now being urged by
35 national and local governments to recycle it and think of waste as a resource. The wheelie-bin culture is being replaced by a series of kerbside collections for paper, metals, plastic, bottles, clothes and compost. The idea is to cut landfill as well as saving the planet. It is, however,
40 having some unexpected consequences. Most of Britain's plastic and paper is now being sent for recycling in China or India, which creates more greenhouse gases just to get it there, plus workers then have to separate it. Meanwhile, some paper and bottles carefully sorted out
45 by householders end up being dumped in landfills after all, because the demand for recycled materials constantly fluctuates.

D Being carbon neutral

If you want to make yourself feel better about the planet, there are lots of ways for you to ease your
50 conscience by becoming 'carbon neutral'. One of the most appealing methods is to pay for someone to plant trees, preferably creating or regenerating new forests. The theory is that trees grow by absorbing carbon dioxide and giving out oxygen, storing the
55 carbon in their trunks. But woods and forests create their own mini-climate, which collects and stores water and creates rainclouds. Added to this, there is the potential problem that planting trees often releases carbon stored in the soil – and what happens if the
60 forests catch fire, or are chopped down and harvested for timber? Another and perhaps better solution might be to invest in small-scale hydro-electric schemes, so that people who live in the Himalayas, for example, and currently do not have electricity, can develop a
65 21st century lifestyle without polluting the planet.

E Eco-tourism

The idea of 'green' tourism is to persuade local people not to chop down forests, shoot elephants or wipe out tigers, but to preserve them so rich tourists visit and peer at the wildlife through binoculars. Unfortunately,
70 the best money is made from reintroducing animals for trophy hunting by the very rich – an idea which does not always meet with approval and has caused much debate. While tourists may help sustain some national parks, they often create as many problems as they solve.
75 One is that they tend to demand all mod cons in their hotels, such as a great deal of water for showers; a luxury sometimes not available for locals. Eco-tourism, when properly managed, can offer the locals and the animals a brighter future. Sometimes, though, the only
80 winners are a few business people who own hotels.

Vocabulary

Meanings of *set*

1 Choose the correct meaning (A–C) of the verb *set* in 1–8.

1 Diana's birthday present was a ruby *set* in a gold ring.
   A organised   B positioned   C marked
2 A deadline for the assignment has not yet been *set*.
   A decided   B regulated   C concluded
3 All questions for the quiz are *set* by experts in their field.
   A studied   B published   C written
4 Leave twenty-four hours for the glue to *set*.
   A harden   B soften   C widen
5 Howard's latest film is *set* in an indeterminate time in the future.
   A comes about   B goes on   C takes place
6 The waitress *set* the dining tables using the best cutlery and crockery.
   A prepared   B placed   C piled
7 Some schools *set* extremely high standards for their students.
   A insert   B expect   C present
8 Our teacher's friendly manner always *set* the tone for her classes.
   A established   B arranged   C insisted

2 Match phrases a–e with 1–5, joining them with the verb *set* in the correct form.

a The writer explained that he …
b To make sure the jelly …
c Since its creation five years ago, the school …
d The company always …
e Unfortunately the date for the reunion …

1 high standards for its teachers.
2 early enough to obtain the preferred venue.
3 job applicants an intelligence test.
4 you need to put it in a cool place.
5 his latest novel in France because he had lived there as a child.

Words with similar meanings (3)

3 Complete sentences a and b with the correct form of the words in 1–3. Use your dictionary to help you.

1 refuse/decline
   a We have to .... your invitation to the opening as we have a prior engagement.
   b Paul .... to admit that he had been the one to cause the accident.
2 refute/reject
   a Despite several job offers, Julia .... them and went back to university.
   b Many people have tried to .... the scientist's theories with opposing evidence.
3 deny/disallow
   a The accused .... being anywhere near the scene of the crime.
   b There were numerous objections from the players when the goal was ....

4 Read sentences a–e below and explain the meaning of the words in italics. Use your dictionary to check how accurate your answers are.

a Could passengers please *ensure* they have all their belongings with them before leaving the aircraft?
b All doors and windows must be *secured* when the building is vacated.
c I was *assured* that the tickets would be delivered on Monday.
d We strongly advise customers to *insure* their possessions when travelling.
e The purpose of this form is to *ascertain* whether you are eligible for the loan you have requested.

Grammar

Emphasis

1 Match a–g with 1–7 to make complete sentences.

a In no way …
b Only when …
c Little …
d Scarcely …
e No sooner …
f Under no circumstances …
g Nowhere …

1 had the boat left the quay than a storm blew up.
2 we opened the front door did we realise that we had been burgled.
3 had the lead marathon runner reached the finishing line when she collapsed.
4 is this newspaper report a true representation of what actually happened.
5 in the city do staff treat you better than in this hotel.
6 did William suspect what lay in store for him.
7 will I ever speak to him again.

Grammar Extra

too and *enough*

2 Rewrite these sentences using the words in brackets.

Example

The sea isn't warm enough for us to go swimming. (too).
The sea is too cold for us to go swimming.

a Pat is too short to be a professional dancer.
(enough) ....
b There aren't enough people using public transport nowadays.
(far too) ....
c The training course is too expensive for most people to consider enrolling.
(enough) ....
d I'm not old enough to drive.
(too) ....
e He spoke too quickly for me to hear what he said.
(enough) ....

3 Insert *too* or *enough* in the correct place in sentences a–h.

a If the tea is not hot, I can make you another cup.
b I'm young to vote in an election this year, but next year I'll be able to.
c There's much poverty in the world today.
d Is there time to look at the shops before we check in?
e Didn't you find that documentary far complicated?
f I'm afraid you are just not studying hard this term.
g Have you really got experience to apply for the job?
h Please speak clearly for everyone to hear you.

Listening Part 4 Multiple matching

1 What are the main environmental concerns in your country?

2 🎧 Listen to five people talking about environmental issues and complete the exam task below.

For 1–5, choose from A–H what the people would like governments to do.

A take action now without having to explain their decisions

B provide more funding for thorough scientific studies

C make sure the information they base decisions on is reliable

D pass laws preventing people from harming the environment

E make sure everyone knows the consequences of international travel

F give more individual responsibilities to specific nations

G help poorer nations become more environmentally friendly

H try to get rid of all threats to the environment

Speaker 1 ☐ 1

Speaker 2 ☐ 2

Speaker 3 ☐ 3

Speaker 4 ☐ 4

Speaker 5 ☐ 5

For 6–10, choose from A–H why the people would like governments to do these things.

A to encourage more students to consider science as a career

B to highlight the harm caused by people's ways of living

C to try to limit the amount of climate change already taking place

D to utilise all available natural resources on the planet

E to find answers to questions we cannot answer at the moment

F to prevent developing nations making mistakes made by other nations

G to avoid making decisions which could have damaging financial results

H to increase the production of cheap types of fuel

Speaker 1 ☐ 6

Speaker 2 ☐ 7

Speaker 3 ☐ 8

Speaker 4 ☐ 9

Speaker 5 ☐ 10

Use of English

Part 1 Multiple-choice cloze

1 Quickly read the text below about plastic bags, ignoring the gaps, and decide who might have written such a text and why.

2 For questions 1–12, read the text again and decide which answer (A, B, C or D) best fits each gap. There is an example at the beginning (0).

SAY 'NO' TO PLASTIC BAGS

Did you know that on **0** ....A.... we take home 150 plastic bags annually? In **1** ...... words, that means a global figure of one million plastic bags taken home every minute. We are sure you'll agree this is a truly shocking statistic.

Plastic bags cannot be simply **2** ...... of along with your domestic rubbish – they can blow off landfill sites and become highly **3** ...... litter which can remain in the environment for a number of years. They are not only an eyesore but they are a **4** ...... to the environment too. For example, plastic bags almost dammed the Buriganga river in Bangladesh, and they are widely **5** ...... responsible for causing devastating floods there on two separate **6** ....

They also **7** ...... a particular threat to wildlife. More and more **8** ...... dead turtles and whales are discovered washed up on beaches, killed by swallowing plastic bags. To marine life, a plastic bag closely **9** ...... a jellyfish.

These are the **10** ...... why you should reuse plastic bags you already have or take a small rucksack on trips to the supermarket. Why not take **11** ...... now and show how much you care about the environment by **12** ...... this small step!

0	A average	B normal	C example	D ratio
1	A fewer	B some	C those	D other
2	A disposed	B thrown	C finished	D used
3	A evident	B observable	C visible	D marked
4	A risk	B danger	C difficulty	D problem
5	A shown	B taken	C made	D held
6	A occasions	B activities	C incidents	D episodes
7	A model	B set	C pose	D generate
8	A repeatedly	B frequently	C usually	D generally
9	A resembles	B reminds	C equates	D appears
10	A motives	B reasons	C sources	D causes
11	A against	B advantage	C action	D account
12	A helping	B doing	C following	D taking

Review Units 10–12

1 Rewrite the second sentence in a–c keeping the meaning the same. Use between three to six words including the word given.

a The Mediterranean is warm, whereas the North Sea is much colder.
  NOTHING
  The North Sea is .... the Mediterranean.

b Tom used to trust Jane, but there's no way he'll ever do that again.
  CIRCUMSTANCES
  Tom used to trust Jane, but .... he ever trust her again.

c I would like to be able to speak Chinese.
  HAD
  I wish I .... to speak Chinese.

2 Write two comparative sentences for each pair of sentences in a–d. Use the words in brackets.
Example
Brass is cheap. Gold is expensive. (nowhere near)
Brass is nowhere near as expensive as gold. Gold is nowhere near as cheap as brass.

a Mexican food is spicy. British food is bland. (far)
b Summer temperatures in France are around 26°C. Summer temperatures in Britain are around 24°C. (only slightly)
c Extreme sports are exciting. Racket sports are boring. (a great deal)
d This exercise is quite difficult. The other exercises are less difficult. (a bit)

3 Put the words in sentences a–e into the correct order. Start with the word in bold.

a long brilliant far was film too **The** but
b allowed **Do** project we to time finish you think enough the have?
c carefully this through haven't enough **We** thought problem
d much has money **The** venture invested company too in already this new
e too application **I'm** arrived be late your for to considered afraid you

4 Complete the paragraph about money with the words below.

  ■ cash   fares   salary   money   change
    wages   bills

There is a saying '1 .... makes the world go round' but whether this is true or not is debatable. What is perhaps true is that our style of living is dictated not by the amount of small 2 .... we have in our pocket but by our annual 3 .... , or the 4 .... we manage to earn on a regular basis. Without those, we wouldn't be able to pay the 5 .... , or afford the 6 .... to get us to work. And if we have nothing in the bank, the 7 .... dispenser is of little use.

5 Combine the two sentences in a–e beginning with the words given.

a James finished cooking dinner. His sister arrived.
  No sooner ....

b He overheard my phonecall to the bank. I didn't know this.
  Little ....

c The plane landed on the narrow runway. All the passengers began to cheer.
  Scarcely ....

d Central Park is beautiful. You won't find a park like this anywhere else in the city.
  Nowhere ....

e There was a cry of protest from the audience. The politician mentioned taxes.
  Only when ....

6 For questions a–c, think of one word only which can be used appropriately in all three sentences.

a Studying abroad didn't .... up to my expectations.
You have to .... life to the full every single day.
It wasn't a pleasant experience, but I suppose we .... and learn.

b I don't .... up to going out this evening, I'm afraid.
The nurse gave him an injection and he didn't .... a thing.
I .... pretty confused about my future at the moment.

c I don't know how Anne .... up with him for so long!
Critics .... his bad performance down to exhaustion.
They're going to .... someone in charge whilst the principal is away.

7 Put the verbs in brackets into the correct form to make suitable conditional sentences.

a Tim often wishes he .... (join) the navy instead of going to work in a bank.

b As long as you .... (not/make a noise), you can watch the film.

c If only the children .... (stop) making so much mess!

d Supposing I .... (tell) you the truth – do you think you would have believed me?

e If I .... (not/drive) so fast the accident might never have happened!

f The meeting will take place unless something unforeseen .... (happen).

8 Write a synonym or explanation for each expression with *set*.

a My sister got a beautiful ring for her birthday – it's a ruby *set* in pearls.

b I'm reading a fascinating novel which is *set* in the eighteenth century.

c The team *sets* high standards for its existing and potential members.

d We haven't *set* a date for our holiday, but it will probably be sometime in June.

9 Complete sentences a–g with *so* or *such*.

a 'Is there any coffee left in the cupboard?'
'I don't think ....'

b The restaurant, ... as it was, closed down last month.

c It was .... an easy exam that I'm sure I've passed!

d Bill reached for a glass on the top shelf. As he did .... , he knocked over a vase.

e My best friend's just bought a new mobile phone. And .... have I.

f We went on holiday out of season .... we could save some money.

g This is .... a complicated instruction manual that I can't understand anything.

10 Choose the correct word to complete sentences a–f.

a The company's representative *denied/refused* to comment on the allegations of fraud.

b Please *ensure/assure* that you switch off your car alarm before leaving your vehicle.

c The results of the research were *declined/refuted* by experts in the medical field.

d Investigators are still trying to *assure/ascertain* the cause of the plane crash.

e The children *denied/rejected* all knowledge of the broken window.

f Ron *secured/assured* his boss that he would do his best to meet the deadline.

Writing

This writing section contains twelve practice tasks for Paper 2 of the CAE exam.

Each task practises the same task presented in the Student's Book and, in most cases, shares the same topic.

For help with the tasks, look back at the Student's Book and refer to the:

- **Writing** section and how to do it boxes in the corresponding unit
- **Writing Guide** on pages 155–165 for model answers and phrase banks

The **Vocabulary** and **Grammar** sections in the Student's Book and the Workbook will help you use a broad range of structures and vocabulary.

Unit 1 Part 2 A formal letter

A friend of yours has decided to apply for the job described below and has asked you to write a character reference for him/her.

Write your **character reference** explaining why your friend would be suitable for the job.

Social Programme Organiser

A well-established language school for international students is looking for someone to organise and run a social programme for students during their free time. If you are:

- energetic
- resourceful
- organised

you may be just the person we need.

Unit 2 Part 2 A proposal

You are on a committee planning a festival in your town. Write a proposal saying what could be included in the festival to best represent your town, and explaining why you think your suggestions would appeal both to local people and visitors.

Write your **proposal**.

Unit 3 Part 1 A formal letter

Your student committee at college has received a memo from the Principal regarding a large sum of money recently made available. You have been asked to write a reply to the Principal. Use the memo and your comments to write your **letter**.

MEMO

TO: The student committee
FROM: M. Wright, Principal

good!

We are fortunate enough to have received a large donation of money and are keen to find out what the students think the money should be spent on. One priority might be new computers and software. Other ideas might be to build a new library, improve sports facilities, or, more controversially, provide money for students wishing to take a year off before starting work. The final decision on how the money will be spent will be made by the board of governors.

Thank you for your help in this matter.

no support for this from students

not necessary — students have computers!

some support

hardly! A great idea!

unfair – why ask us?!

Unit 4 Part 2 A contribution

An international organisation called 'Back to Nature' has asked you to write a contribution to its guide on how people can both appreciate and protect the countryside near where you live. You should include details of interesting places nearby and how people can enjoy visiting them responsibly.

Write your **contribution**.

Unit 5 Part 1 A letter

While studying in England, you spent a weekend with English friends at a caravan site. Read the brochure on which you have made comments. Then write a **letter** to the manager explaining what you found satisfactory, why you were disappointed, and include some suggestions for improvements.

SEAVIEW CARAVAN SITE

LOCATION

yes, but view hidden by trees

Situated in a stunning location, the site is close to the beach and within easy reach of a busy town. *not much nightlife for tourists*

ACCOMMODATION *plenty of space* *didn't work!*

Spacious caravans accommodate up to six guests. All have TV, bathroom, kitchenette, and a sitting area.

true — Attractively decorated throughout.

ON-SITE ACTIVITIES *always busy*

Large sports hall, tennis courts and indoor swimming pool available for guests.

RESTAURANT *not for vegetarians!* *good value for money*

Our on-site restaurant caters for all tastes and includes a fast-food menu.

Unit 6 Part 2 An essay

Your class has had a discussion about the cost of going to university. Some classmates believe the state should have full financial responsibility for students going to university, whilst others think students should make arrangements to pay for it themselves.

Your tutor has asked you to write an essay giving your views on this topic and saying whether you agree or disagree with the points made.

Write your **essay**.

Unit 7 Part 2 A competition entry

You have seen this leaflet announcing a competition in your college.

Competition

Win a day's visit to a well-known national newspaper and find out what it takes to be a top journalist. Just write 250 words on the following subject.

What do you consider to be the greatest problem facing the world today and what can be done about it?

Write your **competition entry**.

Unit 8 Part 2 A magazine article

An international magazine for students has asked readers for articles about the best and worst inventions of recent times. You should describe your favourite and least favourite invention, and say why you have chosen them.

Write your **article**.

Unit 9 Part 1 A report

There has recently been an increase in the number of crimes reported by students at your college. You are the representative for student security. Read the poster outlining safety advice for students, with your comments. Write the **report** outlining your concerns and saying how the college can help.

No one reads posters – get a police officer in to give a talk?

BE SAFE AND SECURE

New students should get a leaflet reminding them to be careful.

Lock it up: most burglaries happen because doors or windows have been left open – always lock your accommodation when you leave.

Money matters: always keep your cash and bank cards safe in a bag or pocket.

As students we simply can't afford to lose money!

Car safety: always lock your car and keep valuables out of sight.

Hardly anyone has a car – more spaces for bikes please!

Bike sense: lock or chain your bicycle – why not have it marked with your name and postcode?

Will the college pay to have our bicycles marked properly?

Close call: keep your mobile phone with you but don't leave it where others can see it.

I've had my phone stolen more than once.

Unit 10 Part 2 A report

You have been asked to write a report for an international company about employment in your country. Your report should say:

- which jobs are most popular with young people in your country and why
- how this compares to attitudes in your parents' generation
- what companies can do to make jobs more attractive to young people

Write your **report**.

Unit 11 Part 2 A review

An international student magazine has asked you to write a review recommending two popular television programmes in your country – one for teenagers and the other for people with a special interest. You should comment on the content and style of each programme, explaining why they are suitable for each group.

Write your **review**.

Unit 12 Part 1 A proposal

You are a member of a student committee at an international college. The Principal has asked the student committee for suggestions for its annual environmental open day. Read the leaflet for last year's open day, on which you have made some notes. Then write your **proposal**.

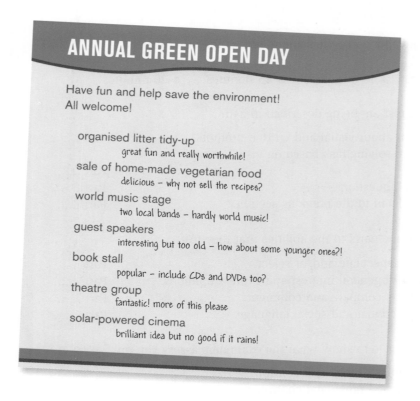

ANNUAL GREEN OPEN DAY

Have fun and help save the environment!
All welcome!

organised litter tidy-up
    great fun and really worthwhile!
sale of home-made vegetarian food
    delicious – why not sell the recipes?
world music stage
    two local bands – hardly world music!
guest speakers
    interesting but too old – how about some younger ones?!
book stall
    popular – include CDs and DVDs too?
theatre group
    fantastic! more of this please
solar-powered cinema
    brilliant idea but no good if it rains!

Part 2 Set text

A book club has asked members to write a short article for its monthly magazine about a character in a book they have read. The title of the article is 'Which character do you most admire and why?' You should briefly outline the plot and then say why your chosen character is the most admirable.

Write your **article**.

Speaking

This Speaking section reviews what you are required to do in the exam and what examiners are looking for. You will listen to CAE students doing Paper 5 Speaking tasks with CAE examiners and under exam conditions. The tasks are taken from the Student's Book and the photos are reproduced here.

The accompanying activities will help you become familiar with the format and requirements of each section. You will be able to assess the students' performances and use these as a model for practising the same tasks yourself.

Listen to the recordings as many times as necessary to do the task.

Quick quiz

1 Does the Speaking Paper carry the same marks as the other Papers?

2 How long is the test? a 10 minutes   b 15 minutes   c 20 minutes

3 Which parts of the test are being described in a–d?

   a   Talk on your own about visual and written prompts.   Part ....
   b   Discuss a problem-solving task based on visual and written prompts.   Part ....
   c   Answer 'personal' questions.   Part ....
   d   Discuss issues related to the previous section.   Part ....

4 Now match each of the parts to the abilities that they test.

   a   Discuss, evaluate, speculate and/or select.   Part ....
   b   Talk about issues of general interest and express opinions.   Part ....
   c   Describe, speculate, compare and comment.   Part ....
   d   Use general interactional and social language.   Part ....

5 Complete the gaps in a–e to show what the examiners assess you on.

   a   G.............. Resource – range and control.
   b   V.............. Resource – range and control.
   c   D.............. M.............. – ability to express ideas in coherent, connected speech without undue hesitation.
   d   P.............. – individual sounds, stress and intonation.
   e   I.............. Communication – initiating, responding and developing the interaction.

Part 1

1   a   Which of these questions would you expect to hear in Part 1?

> Where were you born?   Where are you from?
> How long have you been studying English?   What do you do in your country?
> What are your plans for the future?   What's your favourite time of year?

   b   What answer would you give to the questions in a?

2   🎧 Listen to two extracts from Part 1 and underline the questions (in 1a) the candidates are asked.
What mistakes do the candidates make?

3   a   Which activity does not happen in Part 1?

   ☐ Candidates ask each other questions and interact with one another.
   ☐ The examiner introduces himself/herself.
   ☐ The examiner asks each candidate personal questions.

   b   🎧 Listen and check your answer to a.

   c   🎧 Listen again. Which candidate (female or male) uses better Grammar,
Vocabulary and Discourse Management?

4   What answer would you give to these questions? Think about your Grammar,
Vocabulary and Discourse Management.

> Do you think that having a lot of free time is a good or a bad thing?
> Would you like to spend more time working in another country?

Part 2

1 Complete the format for Part 2 below. You have to ...

  a talk about two .... (what?).
  b talk for .... (how long?).
  c remember the prompts are given on the .... (what?).
  d answer a follow-up question after .... (who?) has finished speaking.

2 a Look at the photos below. Make a list of vocabulary which might be useful to describe them.

> • How might the people taking part in the ceremonies be feeling?
> • How memorable might these occasions be for them?

  b 🎧 Listen to Alborz doing this task. Did he use any of your vocabulary?
    What other vocabulary did he use?

  c 🎧 Listen again. Does Alborz complete the whole task?

3 🎧 Listen to the follow-up question. How well does Yui answer it?

4 🎧 Listen again to both the questions and choose two photos. What answers would you give?

5 Look at the set of photos below. Which of the following phrases could you use to describe them? Can you think of any others?

- period costume
- battle re-enactment
- history books
- other cultures
- early civilisations
- transport yourself into the past
- a crowd of people

6 a Read the task below and choose two photos in 5 to talk about. Take it in turns to do the task. Student A should listen and assess Student B. Points 1–4 will help you. Student B should answer the task. Then swap roles.

> - What can these things teach us about the past?
> - How successfully might they bring the past to life?

1 quickly decide which photos to talk about
2 use a range of structures and vocabulary to compare the photos
3 keep talking despite some hesitation or problems
4 answer the whole task

b 🎧 Listen to Irina answering the task. How does her answer compare with yours?

7 a Read and answer this follow-up question.

"Which way of learning about the past gives the most accurate information?"

b 🎧 Listen to the candidates' answers. How does your answer compare with theirs? Do they manage to keep talking and provide a full answer?

Parts 3 and 4

1 Choose the correct option to complete sentences a–c about Parts 3 and 4.

 a Candidates *must/don't need to* have the same opinions.
 b A conclusion *should/shouldn't* be made immediately.
 c The questions in Part 4 *are/are not* related to the topics in Part 3.

2 🎧 Look at the photos below and listen to two candidates answering a task about staying fit and healthy. Decide if statements a–g are true or false.

 a The candidates waste time thinking about the task before they begin.
 b They interact well with one another.
 c They remember and do the task.
 d They discuss all the photos before making a final decision.
 e They never interrupt or talk over each other.
 f They use a range of vocabulary and structures.
 g They manage to keep talking for the full amount of time.

3 🎧 Listen again and write down the task. Do this task with a partner.

4 What happens in Part 4? Complete sentences a–c.

The examiner will …
a ask questions related to ....
b expect you to express your ....
c not necessarily expect you to agree with your ....

5 a Look at the Part 4 questions below. What answers would you give?

   " How else can you keep fit and healthy?
     Should smoking be banned in all public places?
     Some people say that fast food restaurants promote an unhealthy
     diet. Do you agree? "

   b 🎧 Now listen to the candidates answering the questions. List any useful
   vocabulary they use.

6 a Read the instructions below for another Part 3 task and look at the pictures.
   What answer would you give to this task?

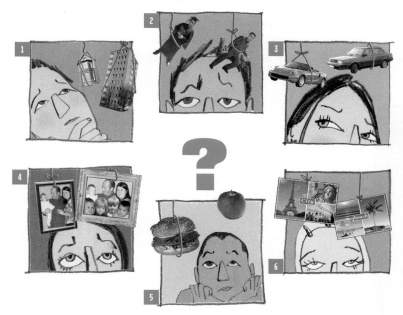

- How difficult is it to make decisions like these?
- Decide which two decisions have the greatest effects on our lives.

   b 🎧 Listen to some extracts from students doing the task in a. Identify the
   techniques used by the candidates in each extract.

   1 developing your partner's ideas   Extract ....
   2 making a comment and encouraging your partner to speak   Extract ....
   3 not dominating the conversation   Extract ....
   4 demonstrating a range of vocabulary   Extract ....

7 🎧 Now listen to candidates doing Parts 3 and 4 of the task and list the questions they
are asked in Part 4. How would you answer these questions?

A complete test

Go to www.oup.com/elt/result and listen to two candidates doing a complete test. Choose an activity from 1–3 below. Then, at another time in your course, choose a different activity and listen again.

The photos for Part 2 are on page 92 and below, and the photos for Part 3 are on page 95.

Look back at the Quick Quiz on page 90 or the previous activities if you need help.

1 a Describe the procedure for each part of the Paper 5 Speaking exam.
   b Make a list of useful advice to remember for each part.
   c 🎧 Now listen to the test. Do the candidates follow the advice?

2 a What five things do the examiners assess candidates on?
   b 🎧 Now listen to the test. Use your assessment guide to rate the candidates' performances in these different areas.

3 a 🎧 Listen and stop the recording after the examiners' questions.
   b What answer would you give to each question? Use the photos to think about useful vocabulary and ideas to discuss. Practise answering the tasks.
   c 🎧 Now listen to the candidates' answers. Did they use any of your vocabulary or ideas?

Part 2

UNIVERSITY *of* CAMBRIDGE
ESOL Examinations

Do not write in this box

Candidate Name
If not already printed, write name in CAPITALS and complete the Candidate No. grid (in pencil).

Candidate Signature

SAMPLE

Examination Title

Centre

Supervisor:

If the candidate is ABSENT or has WITHDRAWN shade here ⬜

Centre No.

Candidate No.

Examination Details

0	0	0	0
1	1	1	1
2	2	2	2
3	3	3	3
4	4	4	4
5	5	5	5
6	6	6	6
7	7	7	7
8	8	8	8
9	9	9	9

Candidate Answer Sheet

Instructions

Use a PENCIL (B or HB).

Mark ONE letter for each question.

For example, if you think B is the right answer to the question, mark your answer sheet like this:

Rub out any answer you wish to change using an eraser.

1	A B C D E F G H		21	A B C D E F G H
2	A B C D E F G H		22	A B C D E F G H
3	A B C D E F G H		23	A B C D E F G H
4	A B C D E F G H		24	A B C D E F G H
5	A B C D E F G H		25	A B C D E F G H
6	A B C D E F G H		26	A B C D E F G H
7	A B C D E F G H		27	A B C D E F G H
8	A B C D E F G H		28	A B C D E F G H
9	A B C D E F G H		29	A B C D E F G H
10	A B C D E F G H		30	A B C D E F G H
11	A B C D E F G H		31	A B C D E F G H
12	A B C D E F G H		32	A B C D E F G H
13	A B C D E F G H		33	A B C D E F G H
14	A B C D E F G H		34	A B C D E F G H
15	A B C D E F G H		35	A B C D E F G H
16	A B C D E F G H		36	A B C D E F G H
17	A B C D E F G H		37	A B C D E F G H
18	A B C D E F G H		38	A B C D E F G H
19	A B C D E F G H		39	A B C D E F G H
20	A B C D E F G H		40	A B C D E F G H

A-H 40 CAS

denote Print Limited 0121 520 5100

DP594/300

UNIVERSITY *of* CAMBRIDGE
ESOL Examinations

Do not write in this box

Candidate Name
If not already printed, write name in CAPITALS and complete the Candidate No. grid (in pencil).

Candidate Signature

Examination Title

Centre

Supervisor:

If the candidate is ABSENT or has WITHDRAWN shade here

Centre No.

Candidate No.

Examination Details

0	0	0	0
1	1	1	1
2	2	2	2
3	3	3	3
4	4	4	4
5	5	5	5
6	6	6	6
7	7	7	7
8	8	8	8
9	9	9	9

Instructions

Use a PENCIL (B or HB).
Rub out any answer you wish to change.

Part 1: Mark ONE letter for each question.

For example, if you think B is the right answer to the question,
mark your answer sheet like this:

0 [A] [B] [C] [D]

Parts 2, 3, 4 and **5:** Write your answer clearly in CAPITAL LETTERS.

For Parts 2, 3 and 4, write one letter in each box.

0 EXAMPLE

Candidate Answer Sheet

Part 1

1	A	B	C	D
2	A	B	C	D
3	A	B	C	D
4	A	B	C	D
5	A	B	C	D
6	A	B	C	D
7	A	B	C	D
8	A	B	C	D
9	A	B	C	D
10	A	B	C	D
11	A	B	C	D
12	A	B	C	D

Part 2

Do not write below here

13   1 0 u
14   1 0 u
15   1 0 u
16   1 0 u
17   1 0 u
18   1 0 u
19   1 0 u
20   1 0 u
21   1 0 u
22   1 0 u
23   1 0 u
24   1 0 u
25   1 0 u
26   1 0 u
27   1 0 u

Continues over ➡

CAE UoE

DP597/301

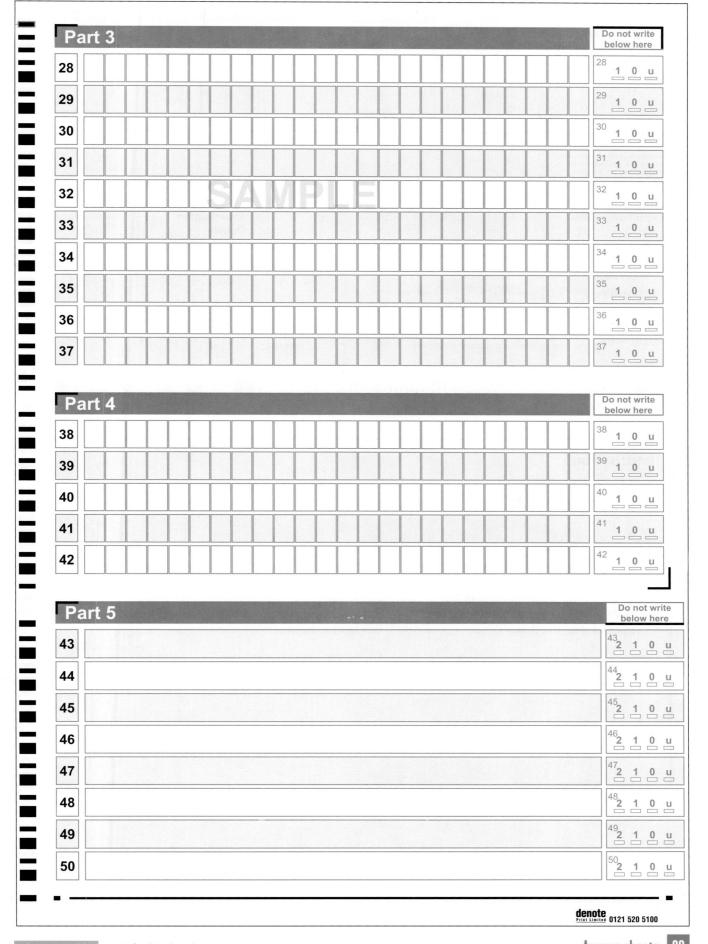

Part 3

Do not write below here

28	28 1 0 u
29	29 1 0 u
30	30 1 0 u
31	31 1 0 u
32	32 1 0 u
33	33 1 0 u
34	34 1 0 u
35	35 1 0 u
36	36 1 0 u
37	37 1 0 u

Part 4

Do not write below here

38	38 1 0 u
39	39 1 0 u
40	40 1 0 u
41	41 1 0 u
42	42 1 0 u

Part 5

Do not write below here

43	43 2 1 0 u
44	44 2 1 0 u
45	45 2 1 0 u
46	46 2 1 0 u
47	47 2 1 0 u
48	48 2 1 0 u
49	49 2 1 0 u
50	50 2 1 0 u

SAMPLE

denote Print Limited 0121 520 5100

Do not write in this box

Candidate Name
If not already printed, write name
in CAPITALS and complete the
Candidate No. grid (in pencil).

Candidate Signature

SAMPLE

Examination Title

Centre

Supervisor:

If the candidate is ABSENT or has WITHDRAWN shade here ☐

Centre No.

Candidate No.

Examination
Details

Test version: A B C D E F J K L M N   Special arrangements: S H

Candidate Answer Sheet

Instructions

Use a PENCIL (B or HB).
Rub out any answer you wish to change using an eraser.

Parts 1, 3 and **4**:
Mark ONE letter for each question.

For example, if you think **B** is the
right answer to the question, mark
your answer sheet like this:

Part 2:
Write your answer clearly in CAPITAL LETTERS.

Write one letter or number in each box.
If the answer has more than one word, leave one
box empty between words.

For example:

| 0 | N | U | M | B | E | R | | 1 | 2 | | | |

Turn this sheet over to start.

Part 1

	A	B	C
1	⬜	⬜	⬜
2	⬜	⬜	⬜
3	⬜	⬜	⬜
4	⬜	⬜	⬜
5	⬜	⬜	⬜
6	⬜	⬜	⬜

Part 2 (Remember to write in CAPITAL LETTERS or numbers)

Do not write below here

7		7 1 0 u
8		8 1 0 u
9	SAMPLE	9 1 0 u
10		10 1 0 u
11		11 1 0 u
12		12 1 0 u
13		13 1 0 u
14		14 1 0 u

Part 3

	A	B	C	D
15	⬜	⬜	⬜	⬜
16	⬜	⬜	⬜	⬜
17	⬜	⬜	⬜	⬜
18	⬜	⬜	⬜	⬜
19	⬜	⬜	⬜	⬜
20	⬜	⬜	⬜	⬜

Part 4

	A	B	C	D	E	F	G	H
21	⬜	⬜	⬜	⬜	⬜	⬜	⬜	⬜
22	⬜	⬜	⬜	⬜	⬜	⬜	⬜	⬜
23	⬜	⬜	⬜	⬜	⬜	⬜	⬜	⬜
24	⬜	⬜	⬜	⬜	⬜	⬜	⬜	⬜
25	⬜	⬜	⬜	⬜	⬜	⬜	⬜	⬜
26	⬜	⬜	⬜	⬜	⬜	⬜	⬜	⬜
27	⬜	⬜	⬜	⬜	⬜	⬜	⬜	⬜
28	⬜	⬜	⬜	⬜	⬜	⬜	⬜	⬜
29	⬜	⬜	⬜	⬜	⬜	⬜	⬜	⬜
30	⬜	⬜	⬜	⬜	⬜	⬜	⬜	⬜

denote Print Limited 0121 520 5100

Key

Unit 1

Reading

1 c

2 1 C 2 B 3 C 4 A 5 D

Vocabulary

1 Positive: confident, cheerful, optimistic
Negative: depressed, fed up, moody, pessimistic
Neutral: curious, resolute, realistic
a fed up
b pessimistic
c positive/optimistic
d confident
e realistic
f moody
g curious

2
a extract or obtain more from
b avoid doing something
c understand
d nearly
e becoming
f have a good relationship
g began
h achieving nothing

3
a get on with
b get down to
c getting us nowhere
d getting on for
e get more out of
f get
g get out of

Grammar

1
1 A: to buy   B: changing
2 A: making   B: spending
3 A: giving   B: seeing

4 A: receiving   B: not informing
5 A: boasting   B: mention
6 A: commuting   B: to look for

2
a enter   e to provide
b to accept   f to solve
c to complete   g to strike
d feel

3
a 2 for forgetting
b 4 of stealing
c 7 for not panicking
d 1 from smoking
e 3 for not living up to
f 5 from rushing
g 6 of travelling
(*at*, *on* and *by* are not needed)

Listening

2 1 C   2 D   3 H   4 F   5 G
        6 D   7 A   8 E   9 B   10 H

Tapescript

Speaker 1
Last month I arranged to go out with my best friend Jenny. At the last minute she rang to say she wasn't feeling well. As luck would have it, I got an unexpected invitation to a dinner party. Imagine my surprise when I walked in and saw her sitting there, socialising with my hosts. I emailed her the next day asking her why she'd lied. In my opinion friends should put each other before anyone else. She replied saying that she didn't have to explain herself to me because our friendship had 'run its course'. I was devastated because I knew then that she just didn't see me as part of her life any more.

Speaker 2
One day my husband was rushed to hospital in another town for an emergency operation. My best friend was very supportive and offered to help when she could but all the others just said they wouldn't be able to. It was funny but the people I almost admired were those who

were prepared to admit that they couldn't help but gave plausible reasons for not being able to do so. I've now come to the conclusion that you can be so-called friends with people for years, but it's all rather superficial. We show other people our lively, desirable selves. So when we suddenly become vulnerable, we turn into people our friends don't recognise.

Speaker 3
I'm one of those guys with a fat address book – maybe because all my friends tell me I'm charming! But as far as I'm concerned, friendship is a club of seven people which was full by the time I was 23. We all share the same interests, and we don't make any demands on one another in emotional terms – which is something I would avoid like the plague. It's not that I don't like making new friends but I just don't need them. We all grew up in the same social, professional and geographical world that we now occupy as adults. The group offers me as much security and intimacy as I require.

Speaker 4
I'm thrilled when I get invitations from new people because you never know who you might meet as a result of them. I make new friends easily but I drop my old ones with equal ease. At the same time, I believe we should be loyal to our friends while we still have them. I think I'm perfectly consistent because in my view, friendships should be automatically dissolved as soon as one participant finds the other boring – from that moment on any demands made on each other should cease. What exasperates me is some people's tendency to keep pursuing me when it's clear the whole thing has come to an end.

Speaker 5
I've been part of a group of friends for quite a few years. Everyone in the group is ambitious and competitive. I can honestly say that my membership of the group has been a greater source of pride to me than my career. But last year I fell out with the most popular couple in the

group and gradually, I sensed that my family and I were being excluded from the group's joint activities. I think what hurt me most was the realisation that even within the group I'd thought of as a refuge, your status inside it was all that counted. No one was prepared to alienate the pair who are the 'leaders of the pack'.

Use of English

1 c

2
1	beneficial	6	professional
2	presentation	7	impression
3	noticeable	8	responses
4	speech	9	revisit
5	orally	10	unease

3 speech

4
- a formal talk given to an audience
- the language used when speaking
- the way in which a person speaks

Unit 2
Reading

1
a The indigenous people of Lapland.
b The separation of the reindeer herds into family groups, according to the signs on the ears of each yearling calf, for the winter grazing.
c He/She was negative about the experience at first, but at the end felt it was a 'privilege'.

2 1 C 2 F 3 E 4 G 5 A 6 D

Vocabulary

1
a imaginative, existing only in the imagination
b exhausting, thorough and detailed
c conscience, doing something thoroughly and carefully
d satisfactory, giving a feeling of pleasure
e sensitive, realistic and practical

2
a	satisfactory	d	conscience
b	imaginative	e	sensitive
c	exhaustive		

3
a	bar	d	mark
b	picture	e	hour
c	data		

Suggested answers
a handbag, handbaggage, handball, handbell, handcuff
b film-maker, film noir, filmstrip
c news agency, newscaster, newsletter
d sideboard, sidecar, sideline, side order
e workbook, work experience, workforce

4 a 2 b 2/3 c 4 d 3 e 1/3/5

5
a	turnout	e	setback
b	takeover	f	turnover
c	breakthrough	g	handover
d	handout	h	breakout

Grammar

1
1	to going	6	on sending
2	on travelling	7	about/of
3	at coping		expanding
4	in wasting	8	in establishing
5	to being		

2
a	2 to convince	d	3 driving
b	5 to resign	e	4 to have
c	1 to be doing	f	6 stealing

3 Suggested answers
a This is the old car **in which** William travelled across Europe.
b The new train, **whose** design is certainly innovative, can reach speeds of 300 km per hour.
c The Welsh mountains, **where** I spent most of my childhood, are very beautiful.
d We met other employees, most **of whom** had been with the company for a few years.
e Winning the World Cup was one of those wonderful moments **when** you feel perfectly happy.
f The film star, **who** will be at the premiere in New York tomorrow, is the subject of much gossip.
g We cannot explain **why** the accident happened.

Listening

2 1 B 2 C 3 A 4 B 5 B 6 A

Tapescript

Extract one
A: I understand that your series of food guides is written to help tourists abroad find places where they can sample the authentic, traditional food of that country?
B: Essentially you're right. But it's a little more than that. Yes, the guides list particular places to eat but I've also included sections on the history of the dishes too – you know, how all the favourite dishes have developed and why, and also how they've changed over the years.
A: Why do you think tourists need a guide like this?
B: A country's food is part of its identity and a visitor to that country should be able to find places where they can eat what the inhabitants eat and in some places observe the customs associated with meal times. You can't find this in the big hotels and restaurants – everything is adapted to the foreigner's taste! That's why my series focuses on the small, difficult-to-find places that the locals go to. I also think it's interesting to learn something about the history of traditional dishes and, for me, the way table manners differ from country to country is quite fascinating.

Extract two
A: It seems strange but one of the most important moments of my childhood was when I discovered the Tooth Fairy didn't exist!
B: The Tooth Fairy?
A: I'm not sure whether this is a British thing or whether other countries have a similar custom. You know, when you're little and your tooth falls out, you put it under your pillow at night and the Tooth Fairy takes it and leaves you some money? Of course, it's your parents really but it's magical for kids.
B: Yes! But you have to be fast asleep in your bed.
A: That's right! My parents were very good at keeping up the custom and for years I believed it. One year, I remember, we were on holiday in Greece and I lost a tooth. I was so worried that the Tooth Fairy didn't work there but she came and left me some money! A few years later, when I found

out it had been my mother all along, I was devastated! I've kept up the tradition with my children though because I think these beliefs are a really important part of your childhood.

Extract three

A: Ayers Rock, or Uluru as the Aborigines call it, is situated in the National Park and is run by the local Aborigines. It is the world's largest single block of stone and has a circumference of eight kilometres. It's considered one of the great wonders of the world. Depending on the time of day and the weather, the rock can dramatically change colour, and it's a very popular place with artists and tourists alike.

B: And can people climb the rock?

A: It can be climbed but not by outsiders. It's all to do with respecting the Aborigines – they believe that the area around the rock is inhabited by their ancestors. They also think that the rock is hollow underground and that it contains a special energy source. They believe that the path up the rock was the traditional route taken by their ancestors and today it is associated with important ceremonies. They also feel they have a duty to ensure the safety of visitors and would feel terrible if anything happened to a tourist while climbing. So, no, tourists don't climb the rock!

Use of English

1 It started when two high school students made six snow statues in Odori Park in Sapporo.

2
1	Despite	9	like
2	itself	10	lot
3	at	11	are
4	has/had	12	which
5	when/as	13	then/after
6	later/on	14	all
7	of	15	such
8	its		

3
a are in favour of observing
b accustomed to being invited
c increase/dramatic rise in attendance (figures)
d to put up with

Unit 3

Reading

1
a Extract from a novel
b Calling all inventors
c Life on Mars

2 1 A 2 A 3 B 4 D 5 A 6 C

Vocabulary

1
a cutback 4   c upbringing 2
b downfall 1   d input 5

2
a over 2   d in 1
b of 6   e down 5
c away 4   f down 3

3 a 2 b 1 c 6 d 5 e 4 f 3

4
a Handing out   d make out
b stand out   e knocked out
c passes out   f turns out

Grammar

1
1 will know/find out
2 has met/meets
3 will perform/is performing
4 knows
5 won't effect
6 will sell out/will have sold out
7 will be given
8 will be talking

2
1 a, b, d
2 c, e, f

4
your opinion fascinating disgusting
size/weight tiny heavy
age young ancient
shape rectangular oval
colour orange purple
country of origin Chinese Russian
material silk china

5
a (On Saturday) spoke (very well) at the conference (on Saturday)
b Christopher probably knows the way to our house. Jane probably doesn't know the way.
c I quite agree with you. I just love your new flat.
d I can see the ship very/pretty clearly on the horizon now.

Listening

2 1 C 2 B 3 D 4 B 5 D 6 A

Tapescript

I: Pete and Sally, we've finally managed to catch up with you before you leave for your trip. So thanks for taking time out to talk to us today. Now, you're about to embark upon a journey of what to most people would be truly epic proportions, aren't you? Tell us a little bit about it.

P: Well, it's certainly an extremely ambitious project. We're travelling through Siberia, through thousands of miles of uninhabited forest – and in winter! But apparently there are fewer swamps then. And it's obviously going to take us a pretty long time – 5 months at least. But what really makes it different this time is that we'll be travelling on two motorbikes.

I: Now all this may sound like a bit of a challenge, to say the least, to most of our listeners, and I'm sure the question they would all like to ask is why are you doing it?

S: We could just say 'why not?' or 'we were feeling a bit bored and were looking for some excitement', but that's not the whole truth of the matter. It's true that one of our aims is to try and raise some money for our favourite charity. But we'd both have to admit that what's really behind it is the fact that it's always been our dream. And if we make it, and we're still speaking to each other at the end of it all, we might even enter the record books as being the first married couple to complete a journey of this kind and still remain friends!

I: Now I know that you've already survived some pretty hazardous conditions on previous trips to Africa and other countries – so how do you feel about what's ahead of you now?

P: Well, there are some stages that are a little alarming to say the least. In fact, it might just prove to be the most perilous journey we've attempted so far. We'll virtually leave civilisation behind to go through some of the most inhospitable terrain in the world. It's a journey that could be full of danger – and who knows what will happen if we break down in the middle of nowhere, especially in such cold conditions.

I: And what do your friends and family make of all this?

S: Those who know something about the terrain we're about to cross have warned us that the journey we're about to embark on will be hazardous in winter. There's the wind chill, not to mention the very real threat of freezing to death along the way. It could all be over sooner than we think if we're not careful! I think some of our friends are a bit dubious about our chances because they've read a lot about winter conditions in Siberia and particularly in the places we're heading for, so they know how bad it can get. But we're trying to stay positive.

I: So what steps are you taking to try and prevent disasters?

P: Well, we've planned very carefully so that food and other basic supplies will all be available en route. In fact, the supply requirement shaped the route itself in detail. We're going to gather enough emergency supplies for up to a week at a time, so we won't starve if we get stranded. What we're doing is enjoying as many hot meals as we can now – just in case we end up having to eat dried food for days which can get very monotonous. We're also trying to prepare for freezing temperatures. Temperatures in Siberia can fall well below those of the Arctic, so we're very aware that frostbite could be a very real concern. Things like wearing inappropriate footwear or not wearing gloves can be fatal in icy conditions. And frostbite can happen very quickly – at any temperature below zero degrees centigrade. However, the lower the temperature, the quicker the damage occurs, and wind-chill factor will increase the risk. So we've invested in specialist clothing specifically designed for the Arctic. That should keep us from harm in the extreme cold.

I: And how often do you plan to have rest periods on the journey?

S: Well, when you're planning a rest stop, you have to watch the weather conditions. Sometimes, it's actually better to keep going than stop and wait for it to pass. But other times, you've got to accept the fact that you can't go on until the weather improves. Even a few inches of fresh snow can make all the difference when you're riding a motorbike, so we're just going to adjust our plans and be flexible.

I: And when it's all over, when do you hope to be heading for home?

P: Not until we've arrived at the most eastern tip of Siberia. After that we'll travel to Hong Kong and fly home from there. But it won't be until we're just about to land at Heathrow that we'll be saying to ourselves: 'We're home, this is it!'

I: Sally, Pete – good luck and we hope to see you again when you're safely back!

Use of English

2 1 A 2 C 3 C 4 B 5 A 6 A 7 D
8 B 9 D 10 C 11 D 12 B

Review Units 1–3

1
a Tim had an extremely fascinating, rather small …
b Did you enjoy yourself at the beach yesterday?
c We found the restaurant pretty easily.
d What a disgusting old oval wooden table!
e I just love your new dress.
f What a dirty, enormous, rectangular pencil case!
g Brenda quite likes being on her own.

2
a workshop   e filmscript
b setback   f side effect
c breakthrough   g turnout
d newsagent

3 a stand   b make   c turned

4
a I showed John the photograph.
b Susie bought her brother a bicycle for his birthday.
c My new car cost me a fortune!
d The authorities insisted on seeing Robert's visa.
e Fetch the visitors some coffee, would you?
f The principal promised the students an extra day's holiday.
g My dentist recommended having two wisdom teeth taken out.
h Be careful not to leave the appliance switched on after using it.

5
a sensitive   d satisfying
b exhausting   e conscientious
c imaginary

6
a would prefer it if
b succeeded in winning
c we recommend washing

7
a input   d cutbacks
b outburst   e upbringing
c downfall

8
a nowhere   d on
b on   e out
c down

9
a where   d why
b whose   e when
c of whom   f of which

10 1 b 2 c 3 c 4 a 5 a

Unit 4

Reading

1
a it has been deliberately sunk and is used for training
b where she first tried diving/ where the introductory course takes place
c someone who is your partner on a dive

2 1 D 2 F 3 A 4 G 5 C 6 E

Vocabulary

1
ive	informative, argumentative, submissive
ious	malicious, mysterious, suspicious
eous	outrageous, advantageous
able	controllable, memorable
ible	forcible, possible, terrrible

2
a outrageous
b argumentative
c suspicious
d informative
e submissive
f malicious
g mysterious
h advantageous
i memorable

Grammar

1
1 have been cutting
2 had previously been covered
3 has now lost
4 have been killed
5 had become/have become
6 has recently been added
7 had never (before) shown

2
	a	b
1	a	no article
2	no article	a
3	no article	the
4	no article	no article
5	The	A
6	no article	A
7	no article	the

3
1	a	6	an	11	the
2	the	7	a	12	-
3	the	8	-		
4	the	9	the		
5	-	10	the		

Listening

2
1 50/fifty
2 brain cells
3 3.2/three point two
4 small head(s)
5 life expectancy
6 rainy
7 insects
8 groups

Tapescript

On our 'Natural World' slot today, we're taking a look at animals in a slightly different light. We humans tend to think we've got it all sewn up when it comes to athleticism, and events such as the Olympics show just what we can achieve. But what we fail to realise is that in terms of real physical abilities, our counterparts in the animal world leave us standing. Let's begin with brute strength. We're all impressed when we watch someone like an Olympic weight-lifting champion hoisting 1.6 times his own body weight above his head. But one tiny ant can make an Olympic champion look positively puny in comparison. The ant can lift a staggering 50 times its own weight – no human could match that. And did you know that each ant has 250,000 brain cells? So a colony of 40,000 ants actually equals one human being in terms of brain cells!

And what about speed? The fastest man on earth broke the 100 metre world record in 9.77 seconds. But we all know the cheetah can beat this with a time of 3.2 seconds. The animals can do this because of their enlarged heart, liver and lungs, which help to deliver bursts of oxygen and energy, and also because of their small head, which offers little wind resistance. But all this fast-living takes its toll and because of this their life expectancy is low, less than ten years in fact, with many cubs never reaching adulthood.

Then there's jumping – 2.45 metres seems to be the best we humans can achieve. The springbok jump not to win a medal but for joy when they're with the herd. During the rainy season, this is particularly common to see and when they do this, it's easy to see how they got their name. The creature can manage a jump of 4 metres from a standing start – they don't even need a run-up to jump five times their own height.

And last but not least, there's shooting. The fastest shooter in the natural world is the archer fish. This extraordinary creature can shoot a 1.5 metre jet out of the water to catch insects. You might argue that an Olympic archer might actually be able to shoot further than his ocean-going counterpart, but he does have to reload more often! And the fish are probably more effective than human shooters because they do it in groups, rather than individually.

So, it looks like we need to organise another competition to run alongside the next Olympic games – namely, the Animal Olympics.

Use of English

1 Patagonia for six weeks

2
1	once	9	hardly
2	deal	10	not
3	was	11	One
4	off	12	her/its/a
5	away	13	first
6	were	14	went
7	us	15	with
8	out		

3 trust

4 a safety   b honesty   c faith

Unit 5

Reading

1
a Roger Bannister ran a mile in three minutes, 59 seconds.
b Bob Beamon set a new record for the long jump of twenty-nine feet, 2½ inches.
c His record was broken.
d Children competed in several sports rather than just one or two.

2 1 D 2 B 3 C 4 C 5 A 6 D

Vocabulary

1
a	hand	e	foot
b	foot	f	head
c	head	g	leg
d	tip	h	fingers

2
a head for
b on the tip of my tongue
c get his head round
d cost an arm and a leg
e give me a hand
f put your foot in it
g foot the bill
h working my fingers to the bone

3
a survivor, survival
b performer, performance
c terrorist, terrorism
d coordinator, coordination
e immigrant, immigration
f defender, defendant, defence

4
a performances
b Immigrants
c terrorism
d defender
e survivors
f coordination

Grammar

1 Suggested answers
1 He said (that) it means (that) he has to keep himself in good physical shape.
2 He told me (that) travelling to remote places …
3 He admitted to always wearing his boots …/He admitted (that) he always wears …
4 He explained that (because) he's very tall …
5 He added that someone in his hut …
6 He went on to say (that) he always carries …
7 He suggested (that) I (could/ should) join him …
8 (But he)/He warned me to keep …

2
a considerate   e known
b natural   f suitable
c correct   g flammable
d compatible

3
a non-violent   e illegible
b impractical   f mistreated
c incompetent   g unsteady
d disconnected

Listening

2 1 C 2 B 3 A 4 C 5 B 6 A

Tapescript

Extract one
A: You also released a fitness video a few years back, Mary, is that right?
B: That was just after I'd finished filming *The Planet*.
A: Did you enjoy making the video?
B: I loved it! I know it seemed to be the 'in' thing to do at the time – just about everyone was releasing fitness videos. But actually sport and exercise were my first loves! I was a serious athlete long before I went into films. So it was a project that was close to my heart.
A: Well, it was certainly the most successful video of its kind at the time.
B: I'm not sure why it was quite so popular. I think perhaps it was because I connected with the people who were using it. I wasn't trying to be too ambitious or getting them to push themselves too far. I just wanted the people who used the video to have a fun workout when they had the time. It's so important to enjoy keeping fit. Like with everything – if it's a pain to do, you'll find a way to get out of it! Human nature!

Extract two
A: You think people should use lunchtimes as a chance to do something healthy, is that right?
B: Absolutely! It's really important to use lunchtimes profitably – to recharge our batteries for the afternoon ahead.
A: And what would you suggest?
B: One of the best things we can do is to get out of our workplace and have a change of scene. Going for a walk outside is an obvious activity. Get out in the park and get some fresh air in your lungs and sunshine on your skin. Believe it or not our bodies physically need sunshine, and lack of it can affect us mentally as well – sometimes leading to depression. And taking a brisk walk every day, even for 20 minutes, can help prevent back problems occurring. This is becoming more common these days as we're spending so much time inactive, sitting at desks and working on computers.
A: And what if the weather's bad?

B: The important thing is not to just flick through a magazine – do a crossword or a word game – it's great exercise for the brain.

Extract three
A: Quite honestly, I think this campaign for healthy school dinners has been a disaster.
B: That's putting it rather strongly isn't it? It must have had some positive impact, surely?
A: Not as far as I can see. I know in theory it is a good idea and something has to be done to encourage children to adopt healthier eating habits.
B: Exactly. And now in school cafeterias there isn't a burger in sight! Junk food has disappeared and in its place the kids can eat salads, vegetables, fruit…..
A: That's all very well and good, but look at all the food school cooks are throwing away every day – it's scandalous! Cafeterias are empty and the children are going to the fish and chip shop in their lunch breaks. How healthy is that?! The problem is that the whole campaign went too far, too quickly. Neither the cooks nor the kids were prepared for the change – which you've got to admit has been pretty dramatic!
B: You think we should go back to burgers on the menu?
A: Not at all. We just need to go more slowly.

Use of English

1 b

2
1 effectively   6 difficulty
2 membership   7 reduction
3 findings   8 beneficial
4 productive   9 critics
5 energetically   10 intensity

3 exercise

4 story

Unit 6

Reading

1 disappointed

2 1 B/E 2 B/E 3 F 4 A 5 C 6 D/E
7 D/E 8 B 9 D 10 B/C 11 B/C 12 E

Vocabulary

1 1 A 2 B 3 C 4 C 5 A

2 1 a giggle, b snigger
2 a mumble, b whisper
3 a overhear, b eavesdrop
Suggested answers
1 unpleasant
2 only a few people can hear
3 secretly listen

3 a eavesdropping
b giggled/were giggling
c mumble

5 1 responsible
2 for questioning
3 my attention
4 extreme views
5 a party
6 the line

6 a 6 b 2 c 3 d 1 e 4 f 5

Grammar

1 a shouldn't   e might
b must   f can't
c should   g ought to
d must

2 b can't have received
c might have been delayed
d may have missed
e must have done
f can't have been

3 a 2 b 3 c 1

4 a needn't have worried
b needn't pay
c needn't arrive
d needn't have spent

Listening

2 1 C 2 B 3 E 4 F 5 A 6 C 7 F
8 E 9 G 10 A

Tapescript

Speaker 1
Apparently in the 1950s, they carried out a series of studies in America that showed that going without breakfast made you less efficient during the late morning. For years afterwards, this was never challenged until a closer study of the original research showed that the findings hadn't really been proved. More recent research shows that going without breakfast has no measurable effects on the body at all, either mentally or physically. It seems that breakfast is simply a matter of personal preference. And for me, I really need regular meals, starting with breakfast. I burn up so much energy during training that I need to have some food there!

Speaker 2
Lots of my clients ask me about the old saying that carrots help you to see in the dark. Well, I can assure you that really poor eyesight can only be helped by wearing glasses or having some sort of surgery. It has very little to do with nutrition. But it is true that if you're short of vitamin A – something which is rare nowadays – you don't see well in dim light: let's face it, no one can see in the dark! And because carrots contain carotene which can be converted to vitamin A, they can make up for this deficiency, but if you've already got enough vitamin A then carrots won't make any difference at all. I could easily recommend more effective supplements.

Speaker 3
Do you remember that cartoon character, Popeye, who ate spinach to get super strength and huge muscles? Parents used to tell their kids to do the same because it would make them strong! Well, there is some truth in it because spinach is packed with iron – a nutrient which is stored in the muscles. The vegetable can be eaten raw but it's actually more nutritious when cooked. It's something I usually try to have on the menu and customers love it! What most people don't realise, though, is that to get the most out of its rather bitter leaf, you

should eat it with a fruit or vegetable rich in vitamin C to increase its iron absorption like oranges or red peppers.

Speaker 4
When I was a child and I had a cold, my mother used to say 'feed a cold and starve a fever.' I personally don't think there's any real cure for sniffly viruses, other than going to bed and waiting until they disappear. I know the doctors in our practice give out that advice all the time. But I read in a magazine in the waiting room, that according to Dutch researchers there is some truth in this old wives' tale. They've found that eating a meal boosts the immune system that destroys viruses, and that includes those that cause colds. What they haven't discovered is whether particular foods have beneficial effects. But, come to think of it, it is true that when you have a fever, you just don't feel like eating at all.

Speaker 5
I've never been that keen on fish but I was told that it makes you more brainy, so I always forced myself to eat it at exam time! And I have to admit that it's one of those things that I find myself saying to my pupils when their exams are approaching. I have read, however, that oily fish like mackerel, pilchards, herring and sardines – all good sources of omega-3 fats (which of course don't make you fat) – does play a role in the development of the brain both before birth and during the first nine months of our life. So if you're one of these people who loves fish, the good news is that it can continue to help your brain function throughout your life. Thankfully for me though, it doesn't actually improve your intelligence, so I don't have to eat it!

Use of English

1 He wants to erect a giant mirror on a mountain to reflect sunlight into the village from November to February.

2 1 C 2 B 3 A 4 D 5 B 6 A 7 C
8 B 9 D 10 C 11 B 12 C

Review Units 4-6

1
a put my foot in it
b head for
c give me a hand
d working your fingers to the bone
e It's on the tip of my tongue

2
The students **became** aware …
when they **started** some research …
It **appeared** that the lynx **had been**
threatened … their numbers **have
been** greatly depleted and their
natural habitat **has been** decreasing.

3
a counterfeit   d take
b count   e whispering
c eavesdropped on f giggling

4
a count   b observed   c held

5
a unsteady
b non-violent
d imprecise
f unnatural
g disorganised
h misunderstood
i mispronounced

6
Jane Henley **could not have been**
happier … Her parents **must** have
been … It **can't** have been … they
needn't have **worried!**

7
1 A: no article
  B: no article, no article
2 A: no article, the
  B: no article, a
3 A: the, the, the
  B: the
4 A: no article, the
  B: no article
5 A: no article, the
  B: the
6 A: no article
  B: the
7 A: a
  B: the
8 A: the
  B: The

8
suspicious, informative, courteous,
malicious, outrageous
a courteous
b informative
c malicious
d suspicious
e outrageous

9
Suggested answers
a Sarah admitted that ever since
  she had been a child, she had
  been desperate to travel.
b She asked Ted if he had ever
  been on a safari.
c He told her that he hadn't.
d But added that it was one of his
  ambitions.
e She went on to say that she
  hoped (that) one day he would
  go on a safari.
f She offered him a place on her
  next trip.

10
a offered to give me/said he
  would give me
b was taken in by
c get my head round

Unit 7

Reading

1
1 c   2 b   3 a

2
1 B   2 A   3 D   4 B   5 C   6 D

Vocabulary

1
1 cut off   4 called off
2 bring … off   5 took off
3 showing off

2
a 4   b 2   c 5   d 1   e 3

3
1 take it in   4 brought in
2 show … in   5 cutting in
3 called in

4
a 4   b 2   c 1   d 5   e 3

5
a off   b in   c off   d in   e in

Grammar

1
1 Lying
2 being located/located
3 Buried
4 Receiving
5 not seeing/not having seen
6 known
7 searching

2
a ee
b ship
c ess (actress)
d hood (likelihood)
e ness (happiness)
f ist
g less/ful
h ese (Chinese, Portuguese,
  Lebanese)

3
Group g can take *less* and *ful*.

4
a politician   g Democracy
b contentment   h argument
c anxiety   i technician
d musician   j secrecy
e clarity   k authenticity
f fulfilment   l diplomacy

Listening

1
a manuscript
b Gluck

2
1 extra cash
2 fake
3 decades
4 blue
5 auction house
6 own hand
7 grandfather
8 generation

Tapescript

Searching dusty attics for hidden
treasures has become a national pastime
in some countries, no doubt encouraged
by the popularity of many TV antique
programmes or just the desire to make
some extra cash! All of us are becoming
increasingly aware that items we've
found may actually be quite valuable
or at least worth more than just a few
pounds. People everywhere it seems
are clearing out their attics, cupboards,
garages, wherever, and taking what they
find to be valued. The upside of this
is that there are a lot of tidy houses!

But what have you really found? Is that picture you're convinced is a Rembrandt really a Rembrandt? The downside of all this searching is that it could result in finding a fake and nothing more. However, having said that, some people do strike lucky. Back in 1990, a librarian in southern California was clearing out her attic when she discovered the original first half of Huckleberry Finn by Mark Twain! The story goes that a set of old trunks, full of paper, had been sitting in her attic for decades. She had inherited them from her aunt but had never got round to investigating them. So, one day she finally decided to get rid of all the clutter and while checking through the trunks she found a fragile package wrapped in brown wrapping paper. On opening it she found lots of blue paper covered in writing in black and purple ink. It was the original manuscript of Huckleberry Finn, well, the first half anyway. I imagine the librarian nearly passed out!

So, what would you do in this situation? The librarian contacted the world-famous auction house Sotheby's and faxed them copies of the pages. Sotheby's then confirmed the find and they had it rushed to New York in an armoured car! They were ecstatic! The manuscript, totalling 665 pages, contained passages not included in the final version of the book and corrections, all of which were written in Mark Twain's own hand. They called it 'the most extraordinary literary discovery of the post-war period'.

The history of the manuscript was traced. It seems that Twain had sent the manuscript to the librarian's grandfather, James Gluck, who was a collector of original manuscripts. They found a letter acknowledging receipt of the manuscript. Unfortunately Gluck caught pneumonia a short time after receiving it and died. Upset by his death, the family packed away all his papers without checking through them. They were eventually inherited by one of his daughters and stored in trunks in her attic until the next generation and the librarian eventually made the find. So, there are treasures out there – amongst all the rubbish and the clutter. Keep looking. Who knows what you'll find?

Use of English

1 He was the first Chinese emperor and arranged for the Army to be built.

2
1 emperor
2 accidentally
3 excavations
4 burial
5 assassinate
6 arrangements
7 warriors
8 unmistakable
9 likeness
10 continuous/continual

3 power

4 back

5
a an attractive body
b is laughed at by others
c is important and influential

Unit 8

Reading

1 To make wisecracks and puns and tell jokes. It needs a lot more development and is not yet successful.

2 1 D 2 B 3 A 4 C 5 B 6 D

Vocabulary

1 a 4 b 1 c 5 d 3 e 2
Suggested answers
self-motivated, self-opinionated, self-righteous, self-service, self-sufficient

2
a full-time/part-time
b left-handed
c light-hearted
d narrow-minded
e handmade

3 b in   c im   d ir   e in
f un   g im   h un

4 1 e 2 g 3 f 4 h 5 c 6 b 7 a 8 d

5
a indistinguishable
b unsocial
c unbearable
d inaccessible
e sensitive/insecure
f irreversible/unchangeable
g immeasurable
h insensitive/uncaring

Grammar

1 Suggested answers
a will hear
b hadn't taken/tried to take
c could call
d could reach
e might be able to find

2
a If my aunt hadn't lent me the money, I wouldn't have been able to go abroad.
b If you stay out in the midday sun, you'll get burned.
c If Thomas hadn't had three jobs over the summer, he wouldn't have been able to buy a motorbike.
d If I were to offer you a scholarship, how would you feel about it?
e If demand for our products were not falling, profits would not be down.

3
a ignites/is ignited, goes up/will go up
b knew, would tell
c would have gained, had volunteered
d hadn't been, would have left
e Let, 'd like
f hadn't worked, wouldn't have got

Listening

2 1 B 2 D 3 C 4 B 5 C 6 D

Tapescript

I: Today we have in the studio Paul Williams – who's an expert in artificial intelligence, or 'AI', as it's often referred to. Paul, welcome. Let's start with a forward-looking question. How difficult do you think it is to predict the future of artificial intelligence?

Paul: Well, I think I'll answer that one by actually looking backwards. It's interesting that in the 1940s, a man called Thomas Watson, who was head of the company IBM at the time, famously predicted that the world demand for computers might actually be as many as five. And in the 1950s, AI researchers predicted that a computer would be the world chess champion by 1968 – but it took a few more decades than that. So AI has certainly had its share of wacky predictions!

I: But leaving aside the predictions of the past, what would be your appraisal of AI's future now?

P: As you might imagine, there's still a lot of controversy about all this. But basically, most experts remain optimistic about its future. Nevertheless, they're currently predicting that it won't be until the middle of this century that intelligent machines will dominate every area of our lives.

I: OK. So what impact is AI already having on our lives?

P: That's actually an interesting question and people may be surprised by the answers. There are already so many examples of the impact AI is having on our technology. Every call on your mobile and every email you send is routed using AI. And there are many other examples of what you would call 'narrow AI' – that is something which can now be done by a computer, but used to be done by a human. It's called 'narrow' because it is within a specific area, but it's actually getting wider – slowly, but it is getting wider.

I: So is this an unprecedented leap forward, or are there any other examples of similar kinds of technology which have had this kind of effect on our lives?

P: Some people would say that the best comparison is probably that AI is at the same stage now as the personal computer industry was in 1978. The Apple II came out the year before and Atari had just brought out the 400 and 800 models. So there wasn't a lot of choice if you wanted to buy one. And, obviously, they couldn't do as much as today's computers do. But my take on the situation is that the comparison with the early computer industry doesn't give a true picture of AI's successes. It's already used in very advanced ways, like

scheduling flights or reading X-rays. The stereotypical image of AI – like Commander Data in *Star Trek* and David in the film *AI* – is not that far away.

I: What might that mean exactly?

P: Well, I'll stick my neck out and say that probably in the next few decades we'll have a better understanding of how the human brain works. That will give us a sort of template to follow and it'll really help in developing AI. That would mean that within the next fifty years, there'll be a lot of intelligent robots. You may say that it all sounds a bit far-fetched, but take a moment to think back to the 1900s. Who would have thought a century later, it would be normal to have computers in your home – and I'm not just talking about laptops or personal computers. You only have to look at the computer chips in our coffee makers, refrigerators, ovens and radios to see the kind of unexpected leaps that took place.

I: So should we be afraid of what these intelligent machines might eventually do to us?

P: I must admit that the thought of a hyper-intelligent coffee maker trying to kill us all in our kitchens does seem a little too far-fetched! What we should perhaps be more worried about is whether we humans will be made redundant by a legion of intelligent machines. But the simple answer is that we won't wake up one morning to find our lives populated with all manner of artificially intelligent devices.

I: How can you be so sure?

P: Well, science fiction is just that – fiction; it's not based on fact. Spielberg's *AI* may have had a company designing a robot that could bond like a child or human, but that was in a film. But scientists don't just suddenly decide to make an emotional, human-like robot. Things don't happen that way. However rapid the advance of technology, the advent of AI will be a gradual process. The road from here to the real application of artificial intelligence will take thousands of different routes. There's really no need to panic.

I: Paul, thanks very much for talking to us today – and now for …

Use of English

1 People want to get onto a course or into a workplace, and to develop 'soft skills'. Businesses want to raise their profile in the community.

2 1 A   2 D   3 B   4 C   5 D
   6 A   7 B   8 C   9 C   10 A
   11 B   12 A

Unit 9
Reading

1 A   Scotland   D   USA
   B   England   E   England
   C   Cuba   F   USA

2 1 D/F 2 D/F 3 A 4 C 5 F 6 E 7 C
   8 F 9 A/B/F 10 A/B/F 11 A/B/F
   12 A/E 13 A/E 14 B 15 D

Vocabulary

1 a for   e behind
   b back on   f off
   c over (oneself)   g out with
   d through

2 1 fallen behind
   2 falling over themselves
   3 fall back on
   4 fell through
   5 fell out
   6 fell for
   7 fallen off

Grammar

1 Bowlands Academy of Arts was established five years ago. The establishment has now been officially recognised by the Department of Education. A programme of short, intensive courses, as well as three-year degree courses, are offered to students. A range of examinations

can be taken (by students) throughout the year. Students are instructed in small groups (by staff) and a personal tutor is assigned to every student. Accommodation in a hall of residence must be booked in advance (by anyone requiring it). A deposit needs to be enclosed with the enrolment form. The balance will be requested (by the Academy) before the course starts. The Academy needs to be informed immediately if students intend to withdraw from their course.

2
1 get your eyes tested
2 had her ears pierced
3 get the/your jacket dry-cleaned
4 get confiscated
5 had the car serviced
6 doesn't get stolen
7 am having the matter investigated

3
a It is rumoured that the government is going to resign.
b Interest rates are predicted to rise by financial experts.
c The missing gangland leader was assumed to have been murdered.
d It is thought (that) the plane crash was due to human error.
e Terrorists are believed to be hiding out in the north of the country.

Listening

2 1 A 2 B 3 C 4 A 5 C 6 B

Tapescript

Extract one
A: This new punishment policy seems to be succeeding but it has certainly attracted a lot of media attention.
B: Yes – that's true. There's been a fair amount of controversy surrounding it. But there will always be people for and against different forms of punishment. This particular idea is proving very effective.
A: Why do people call it 'the cooler room'?
B: Well, it's an isolation unit and I suppose people see it as a place for schoolchildren to cool off. 'The cooler room' also featured in the film The Great

Escape where it was a room used to punish the prisoners.
A: So, what happens in 'the cooler room'?
B: Disruptive pupils are sent there to do work away from their friends and they aren't allowed to leave without permission. Food and drink are brought into the room and they're constantly observed through a window. They can be sent there for as little as one hour but for really bad behaviour it can be up to three schooldays! They hate being away from their mates and this is what makes it effective.

Extract two
A: At the time they were introduced, ASBOs seemed a really good idea – a form of punishment that targets people guilty of habitual antisocial behaviour and forbids them to do certain things, associate with certain people or go to certain places. That's got to be better than sending them to prison. Well, that was the thinking anyway.
B: But these recent statistics are pretty alarming, wouldn't you say? It appears that ASBOs aren't having the effect that government thought they would.
A: You're right. What's happening is that a lot of the kids don't actually understand the limitations of the orders and those that do understand don't particularly care. In some cases it's developed into a game to see how often they can breach their order, ignoring all the restrictions, and get away with it.
B: The report says that ASBOs are even seen as a 'badge of honour'.
A: I know! Rather like a symbol – something to show off about and be proud of. So, you see in one way they're encouraging antisocial behaviour rather than discouraging it!

Extract three
A: Could you tell our listeners exactly what the Witness Support Programme does?
B: Certainly. We do a lot of different types of work but mainly we're concerned with supporting people who have been victims, or witnesses, to crimes. In particular, we help when cases go to trial and they are required to attend court to give evidence.
A: And why do these people need help at court?
B: You can imagine the trauma they have suffered, then having to relive this and describe what happened when they give

evidence. Standing up in court can be an unnerving experience. We try to make it less stressful. We bring them to the court, prior to the trial, to familiarise them with the surroundings and the procedures. Then, during the trial, we provide a separate room away from the public and the risk of meeting the friends and family of the accused person.
A: This support programme is a charity, isn't it?
B: Yes. In this area, three of us are paid to organise everything but we depend on large numbers of volunteers who help the witnesses along the way.

Use of English

1 crime/drama/thriller

2
1	in	9	Each
2	are	10	what/as
3	who	11	to
4	about	12	the
5	own	13	which/that
6	of	14	itself
7	one	15	be
8	from/by		

3
a chances are (that) you won't
b falling over himself
3 being/going to be looked into

Review Units 7-9

1 1 d 2 e 3 c 4 b 5 c/d 6 c

2
1 Having peered
2 Using
3 identifying
4 known
5 making
6 Having concluded

3
a fallen for
b fall behind
c falling over themselves
d fell through
e fell out
f fall for

instead of looking at it.

Don't forget that art is, in some cases, priceless, and its protection is a very serious issue for galleries. Security is therefore strict – avoid leaning over the ropes; if you get too close to the art, the security guards might throw you out of the art gallery. And no matter what you do, never touch the art unless a sign specifically says you can. Remember that it's an art gallery, and you may harm the work you touch.

I know it sounds ridiculous, but take a pair of binoculars. Art galleries with special 'for a limited time only' displays can get very crowded. Sometimes you can get a better view by standing back and looking through binoculars than you can by trying to wrestle your way to the front of a crowd of schoolchildren.

Don't waste time in front of mediocre works. Look for something unusual. Even in the best gallery, not everything is great. And if it doesn't interest you, keep going until you do find something unusual. And if someone asks you why you don't like a painting, just say something like, 'the artist obviously didn't take into account the subject's emotional state'. Nobody will argue.

So that's it. If you commit all this to memory and remember it the next time you go to a gallery, you'll be able to appreciate art – and maybe even teach other people a thing or two.

Use of English

2
1	about	9	with
2	just/only	10	up
3	having	11	how
4	from	12	as
5	more/most	13	would
6	any	14	so
7	like	15	another
8	take		

3
a got round to finalising
b in the event of
c managed to get away with/got away with
d went on to become/be

Unit 12

Reading

1 c

2 1 E 2 D 3 B/C 4 B/C 5 B 6 C 7 A
8 C 9 A/E 10 A/E 11 D 12 B

Vocabulary

1 1 B 2 A 3 C 4 A
5 C 6 A 7 B 8 A

2
a 5 had set/set   d 3 sets
b 4 sets   e 2 wasn't set
c 1 has set

3
		a		b	
1	a	decline	b	refused
2	a	rejected	b	refute
3	a	denied	b	disallowed

Grammar

1 a 4 b 2 c 6 d 3
e 1 f 7 g 5

2
a Pat is not tall enough to be a professional dancer.
b There are far too few people using public transport nowadays.
c The training course is not cheap enough for most people to consider enrolling.
d I'm too young to drive.
e He didn't speak slow(ly) enough for me to hear what he said.

3
a If the tea is not hot **enough** …
b I'm **too** young …
c There's **too** much poverty …
d Is there **enough** time …
e … far **too** complicated?
f … studying hard **enough**
g … **enough** experience to …
h Please speak clearly **enough** …

Listening

2 1 C 2 E 3 B 4 D 5 G
6 G 7 B 8 E 9 C 10 F

Tapescript

Speaker 1
Of course I'm not going to deny that governments have a huge responsibility to protect the planet. But the single, most important statement I would like to hear governments making is that the science of global warming is not an exact one – not as long as various methods of measuring temperatures give contradictory results. Over the last 25 years, weather satellites have shown little, if any warnings, and computer models used to predict future temperatures and other climate effects have produced completely different predictions that can't be relied on. It would be crazy to use inaccurate information as a basis for policies that could have an effect on national economies.

Speaker 2
The one measure I would like to see governments agreeing on and promoting would be to introduce legislation forcing producers and manufacturers to clearly show the environmental cost of transporting goods. Consumers everywhere should be able to see at a glance exactly what they're doing to the environment by flying in a plane, for example. Showing people that they can make different lifestyle choices and purchases is one essential step towards reflecting the damage to the environment. So, the environmental damage caused by transporting, say, fresh fruit and vegetables around the world should be made clear – just like the damage caused by taking a package holiday and flying to your destination. It's only by doing this that you can make people realise the short and long-term effects of what they're doing.

Speaker 3
It's my opinion that decisions regarding climate change must continue to be based on good science. Science has already demonstrated that climate change is happening – but there are still many unanswered questions that need detailed scientific research. These include: What are the likely environmental and human impacts? What exactly are the regional changes going to be? How are extreme events going to change, for example, flooding, heat waves and drought? These questions can only be answered through continued

coordinated research using the latest computer technology. And that costs money. So my request would be that governments invest much more in doing research in this field.

Speaker 4

My worry is that governments are not focusing enough on adaptation. True, they all make statements about cutting greenhouse gas emissions. You read something about it every day in the press. But what they fail to realise is that climate change is occurring and it's going to carry on occurring even if we do cut emissions. We already know that sea levels are rising and there are heatwaves now in countries like the UK. So what I want governments to do is admit that they need to bring in global legislation which will help to minimise what is going on at this moment in time.

Speaker 5

The point is that the developed world created the present problems with the environment as it became industrialised and wealthy. So I think that governments have to recognise the fact that developing countries will need more energy as their standards of living rise – and that if those needs are met in the easiest and cheapest way, their greenhouse gas emissions would be enormously high. And any financial savings that the developed world might make would result in even greater pollution. So we have an obligation to help developing countries avoid a repetition of what happened to us. And the developing countries must play their part in protecting the planet as their economies grow.

Use of English

1 Suggested answers
an environmental group/local recycling group/supermarkets, to encourage people to reuse plastic bags and avoid unnecessary waste

2 1 d 2 a 3 c 4 b 5 d 6 a
  7 c 8 b 9 a 10 b 11 c 12 d

Review Units 10-12

1 a nothing like as warm as
  b under no circumstances will
  c had the ability

2 a Mexican food is far spicier than British food./British food is far more bland than Mexican food.
  b The summer temperature in France is only slightly warmer than it is in Britain./The summer temperature in Britain is only slightly colder than it is in France.
  c Extreme sports are a great deal more exciting than racket sports./Racket sports are a great deal more boring than extreme sports.
  d This exercise is a bit more difficult than the others./The other exercises are a bit less difficult than this exercise.

3 a The film was brilliant but far too long.
  b Do you think we have allowed enough time to finish the project?
  c We haven't thought this problem through carefully enough.
  d The company has already invested too much money in this new venture.
  e I'm afraid your application arrived too late for you to be considered.

4 1 money 4 wages 7 cash
  2 change 5 bills
  3 salary 6 fares

5 a No sooner had James finished cooking than his sister arrived.
  b Little did I know that he had overheard my phonecall to the bank.
  c Scarcely had the plane landed on the narrow runway when the passengers began to cheer.
  d Nowhere in the city will you find a park as beautiful as Central Park/this (one).

e Only when the politician mentioned taxes was there a cry of protest from the audience.

6 a live b feel c put

7 a had joined
  b don't make a noise
  c would stop/had stopped
  d had told/told/did tell
  e hadn't been driving/hadn't driven
  f happens

8 a positioned c enforce
  b takes place d decided

9 a so e so
  b such f so
  c such g such
  d so

10 a refused d ascertain
   b ensure e denied
   c refuted f assured

Speaking

Part 1

1 a all

2 Where are you (both) from?
  What do you do in your country?
  How long have you been studying English?
  I was born in Iran …, everybody asks me if I'm from Tokyo …, I'm from the countryside and there's a totally different atmosphere where I grew up, I was a high school student and graduated and came here to learn English.

3 a Candidates ask each other questions and interact with one another.
  c Male: demonstrates good command of structures and coherence. Female: answers are too short and repetitive.

Part 2

1 a photos/pictures
   b 1 minute
   c sheet/exam paper
   d your partner

2 a Suggested answers: Olympics,
      graduation, proud, achieved,
      studies, represent their country,
      world, memorable, lifetime,
      chance
   c Yes.

3 Poor answer, because she doesn't
   give any reason or expansion.

5 all

7 b Yes, they do.

Parts 3 and 4

1 a don't need to   c are
   b shouldn't

2 true: b, c, e, f, g   false: a, d

3 I'd like you to imagine that the
   government is producing a leaflet
   to help young people stay fit and
   healthy. Here are some pictures
   they are considering including in
   the leaflet. First, talk to each other
   about how successful these pictures
   might be in encouraging young
   people to stay fit and healthy. Then
   decide which one should be on the
   cover of the leaflet.

4 a the topics in Part 3
   b ideas and thoughts
   c partner('s ideas)

5 b have the opportunity,
      workplace, keep a balance,
      meditation, healthy food/diet,
      the pub, respect others, light
      food, junk food, obesity,
      harmful, lose a lot of customers

6 b
   1 Extract 4   3 Extract 3
   2 Extract 1   4 Extract 2

7 So what decisions in life do you
   consider the most difficult to make?
   Some people believe that a lot of
   important decisions are out of our
   hands. What do you think?
   What sorts of decisions in life are
   influenced by money?

A complete test

1 a

   Part 1
   Two-way conversation between
   candidate and examiner. The
   examiner asks each candidate
   personal questions and then
   introduces Part 2.

   Part 2
   Candidates talk about visual
   prompts, then answer a follow-
   up question about their partner's
   pictures.

   Part 3
   Candidates work together to discuss
   a problem-solving task given by the
   examiner and reach a decision at
   the end.

   Part 4
   The examiner asks candidates
   questions related to the topics
   discussed in Part 3.

2 a Grammar, Vocabulary,
      Discourse Management,
      Pronunciation, Interactive
      Communication

3 a

   Part 1
   Where are you both from?
   How long have you been studying
   English?
   Would you like to spend some time
   working in another country?

   Part 2
   I'd like you to compare two of the
   pictures and say how the people
   taking part in the ceremonies might
   be feeling, and how memorable
   these occasions might be for them.
   Which of these occasions do
   you think would be the most
   memorable?
   I'd like you to compare two of these
   pictures saying why the people
   have changed their appearance in
   these ways, and how they might be
   feeling.
   Which change of appearance do
   you think is the most necessary?

   Part 3
   Talk together about how difficult it
   is to make decisions like these, and
   decide which two decisions have
   the greatest effect on our lives.

   Part 4
   What decisions in life do you
   consider the most difficult to make?
   Some people believe that a lot of
   important decisions are out of our
   hands. What do you think?
   What sorts of decisions in life are
   influenced by money?

oxfordenglishtesting.com

What is on the Workbook MultiROM?

The MultiROM in this Workbook Resource Pack has two parts.

- You can listen to the audio material that accompanies the workbook by playing the MultiROM in an audio CD player, or in a media player on your computer.

- You can also access two practice tests online with the MultiROM. Read the next page to find out about test features. To find out how to access them, read this page.

How do I use my MultiROM?

You will find your practice tests on a website called oxfordenglishtesting.com. The website contains many different practice tests, including the ones that you have access to. Because the practice tests are on the internet you will need:

- to be connected to the internet when you use the tests
- to have an email address (so that you can register).

When you're ready to try out your practice tests for the first time follow these steps:

1 Turn on your computer.
2 Connect to the internet. (If you have a broadband connection you will probably already be online.)

3 Put the MultiROM into the CD drive of your computer.
4 A screen will appear giving you two options. Single click to access your tests.

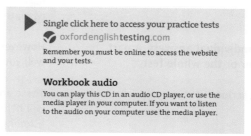

> ▶ Single click here to access your practice tests
> ✓ oxfordenglishtesting.com
> Remember you must be online to access the website and your tests.
>
> **Workbook audio**
> You can play this CD in an audio CD player, or use the media player in your computer. If you want to listen to the audio on your computer use the media player.

What do I do when I get to the website?

After a few moments your internet browser will open and take you directly to the website and you will see this screen. Follow steps 1–3. If the screen does not appear follow step 4.

3 After filling in the registration form click on **Register**. To confirm your registration, click on **Save registration details**. Click on **My tests** where you will be asked to log in. You have one year to use the practice test before you have to submit it for final marking.

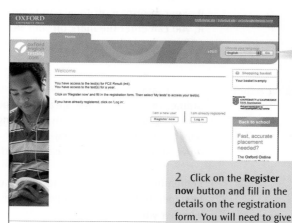

1 Choose a language from the drop-down list and click **Go**. All pages, apart from the actual practice tests, will be in the language you choose.

2 Click on the **Register now** button and fill in the details on the registration form. You will need to give an email address and make up a password. You will need your email address and password every time you log into the system.

4 The website knows which practice tests you have access to because it reads a code on your MultiROM. If the above page does not appear, go to www.oxfordenglishtesting.com/unlock You will be asked to click **Register now** if you are a new user. You will then be asked to fill in a registration form and to enter an unlock code. You can find the unlock code printed on your MultiROM. It will look like this 9219e6-9471d9-cf7c79-a5143b. Each code is unique.

Once you have registered, you can access your tests in future by going to oxfordenglishtesting.com and logging in. Remember you will need your email and password to log in. You must also be online to do your practice tests.

What are the features of each test?

Exam tips	You can see a tip on how to answer every question type.
Dictionary look-up	You can look up the meaning of any word in the practice test. Just double click it and a definition will pop up. You need to have pop-up windows enabled.
Instant marking and feedback	When you've answered a question, you can mark it straight away to see whether you got it right or wrong, and you can get feedback to find out why.
Change your answer or try again	You can then go back and have another go as many times as you like. Understanding why you answered a question incorrectly helps you think more clearly about a similar question next time.
Save and come back later	You don't have to complete a Paper in one go. When you log out it saves what you've done. You can come back to it at any time. You have 365 days before you have to submit the practice test for final marking. The **My tests** page tells you when the test expires.
Mark individual answers, a part, a paper or the whole test	However much you've done of the practice test, you can mark it and see how well you're doing.
Audio scripts	These are available for all parts of the Listening test. Reading the audio script will help you understand any areas you didn't understand when you were listening to them.
Sample answers for essay questions in the Writing paper	You can see *sample answers* after you've written your own. They've been written by real students, and will give you a good idea of what's expected. The essay you write will not be marked automatically. If you would like your teacher to mark it, you can print it off to give to them or email it to them. When they've marked it, you can enter the mark on your **Results** page. It does not matter if you do not enter a mark for the essay. The final marks will be adjusted to take that into account.
Useful phrases for the Speaking paper	You get sample Speaking papers and *Useful language* to help you practise offline. You can print the Speaking paper from the **Learning Resources** page, and ask your teacher to do the Speaking paper with you. As with the Writing paper, you can enter the mark your teacher gives you. However, even if you don't, your final marks will be adjusted to take that into account.
Results page	Remember this is a practice test not the real exam. You will see your score by paper and part and as a percentage. You will only get an indication as to whether your score is equivalent to a pass or not.
Try a sample test first	You can try out a short version of a practice test on oxfordenglishtesting.com before you do a real one. This lets you find out how to use a test before you start.
Buy more practice tests	To get even more practice, you can buy more tests on oxfordenglishtesting.com